James Payn

The Love Songs

James Payn.

The Love Songs

ISBN/EAN: 9783337007034

Printed in Europe, USA, Canada, Australia, Japan

Cover: Foto ©Thomas Meinert / pixelio.de

More available books at **www.hansebooks.com**

THE

LOVE SONGS OF " PODD,"

INCLUDING

SONNETS ON WORCESTER.

BIRMINGHAM :

WHITE AND PIKE, MOOR STREET.

WORCESTER :—DEIGHTON & SON, High Street.
BIRMINGHAM :—CORNISH BROTHERS, New Street.
WOLVERHAMPTON :—BARFORD & NEWITT, Queen Street.

MDCCCLXXXIV.

PREFACE.

COME, maidens fair! come, youths as well!
    And listen to my song;
I'll make you feel your bosoms swell
    With love's flame pure and strong.
I'll make it known how sweet it is
    To roam through mead and grove;
And how sweet vow, and how sweet kiss,
    When breath'd by those we love.

Come, critics, too, and spend your ire,
    And this my work abuse;
My ardour strong will stand the fire,
    Nor hush'd will be my muse.
This breast of mine a sigh may heave
    If slight I get from maid;
But know, it never yet could grieve
    At what a critic said.

Come, stoics, too, and vent your spleen,
    And tell me in one cry
How foolish and how wrong I've been
    For maiden e'er to sigh.
I may be wrong, you may be right,
    I care not which it be;
But what I do is my delight,
    And that's enough for me.

But come, fair maids, for 'tis for you
    That thus my sonnets flow;
For 'twas through you sweet love I knew,
    With all its joy and glow;
And what had been this life of mine
    Unless I had felt love?—
A day that saw no sun to shine;
    A night, no star above;

Instead of this, life has been joy,
    With scarce a pang of woe;
Though he who loves must sometimes sigh,
    And let some teardrops flow.
Yet, even then, to grieve proves bliss,
    For hope will give us cheer,
That we may win again the kiss,
    The loss of which brought tear.

So give me ear, ye lovers true,
    And I will sing my lays,
And deem myself rewarded, too,
    If I but win your praise.
Though keenest critics cry me down,
    And stoics do the same,
Your smiles will bid me hold my own,
    And ward off all their blame.

Songs of Worcester.

I.*

LET gentle spring, with mantle green,
 Make Hallow's meadows fair ;
Let flowers wild deck Henwick's scene,
 And sweetly scent the air :
Let violet blue and primrose pale
 Bloom in green Berwick's wood ;
And bluebells deck each shady dale
 Beside Sabrina's flood ;

Let lark soar high from Cleveload's mead
 And ring his song above ;
Let nightingale her accents plead
 In Kempsey's silent grove.
To me in vain the songsters sing,
 In vain bloom flowers gay :
Those scenes rejoice 'neath gentle spring,
 But I am far away.

Oh, scenes so fair ! Oh, flowers gay !
 Oh, songsters glad and free !
How I do think of ye each day,
 And wish I near could be.
How much I yearn to view each scene,
 And once more roam them o'er,
And view the glories of spring green,
 E'en as I did of yore.

* Berrow's Worcester Journal, April 19th, 1879.

B

II.*

THE sun that basks in Teme is bright,
  The meadows by that stream are fair,
And ever pleasing to the sight
  Of those whose footsteps wander there.

What lark so glad as he that rings
  His song in Newland's azure sky?
What thrush so free as he who sings
  His notes in Ketch or Cleveload nigh?

What blackbird dun hath tone as clear
  As he that trills in Spetchley's brake?
What swallow cleaves the balmy air
  Like that which skims o'er Pirton's lake?

And where the bank that will compare
  To Cliffy by Sabrina's side
When blooms the primrose pale and fair
  And bluebells nod in stately pride?

The buttercup and daisy neat
  Lie thick on Kempsey's open plain;
The modest violet doubly sweet
  In Berwick blooms when spring doth reign.

The cowslip, with its golden crest,
  Makes gay Powick's meadows fresh and green;
The hedgerows, with wild roses drest,
  Make fairer still Croome's pleasant scene.

'Tis true all praise their place of birth,
  And deem it this world's brightest view;
But fairer spot is not on earth
  Than Berwick green or Malvern blue.

* *Worcester Herald*, August 4th, 1883.

III.*

WHO has not wandered by that stream
    Which softly flows 'neath Hallow high?
Who has not rambled by the Teme.
    Whose face reflects Powick's azure sky?
Their waters pierce one mountain's breast †
    In Cambria's ranges wild and vast ;
Yet like two lovers sad and blest,
    Though parted long embrace at last.

Who has not wandered to that spot
    Which sees these sister streams unite ?
There, when the summer's day is hot,
    Blow fragrant breezes, cool and light.
A calmness dwells upon the scene
    Which soothes the restless heart and soul ;
For, while one views the valley green,
    He yields to Nature's soft control.

Oh, where the stream with banks as green
    As Severn wide, or narrow Teme ?
What river flows through fairer scene ?
    What river's ripples brighter gleam ?
Earth may be wide, and many a stream
    May flow unsullied to the sea,
But not where sun or moon sheds beam
    Can there two fairer rivers be.

Worcester Herald, September 1st, 1883.   † Plinlimmon.

WHERE Severn's stream meets wand'ring Teme,
   How fair 'tis there in spring !
How sweet to rove through Kempsey's grove,
   And hear the wild birds sing !
How blue the hills, how clear the rills,
   That Malvern gives to view !
No wonder I should often sigh
   Since I bid them adieu.

No morning grey e'er brings its day
   But in my heart they dwell ;
Nor in the west sinks sun to rest
   But they're remembered well.
The darksome night ne'er wings its flight
   But of those scenes I dream ;
And as of yore I ramble o'er
   Those meadows by the stream.

ONCE more Powick's meadows don their green,
　　And blue looks Malvern sky;
Once more sweet flowers deck Croome's scene,
　　And please the rambler's eye.
Once more soars lark in realms of blue,
　　O'er Kempsey's verdant plain :
And primrose pale, and violet too,
　　In Berwick bloom again.

Once more pipes thrush his happy lay,
　　In Kempsey's shady grove ;
And Cleveload's copse the livelong day
　　Hears wooing of the dove.
Once more in Spetchley's silent brake
　　The blackbird whistles clear ;
And swallows skim its sparkling lake,
　　Or cleave the azure air.

Powick's meads may don their mantle green,
　　And blue look Malvern's sky ;
Buds, too, may beautify each scene,
　　And lark soar singing high ;
The thrush and blackbird sweet may sing,
　　Dove coo, skim swallow gay ;
All these rejoice 'neath gentle spring,
　　While I sigh far away.

VI.

I LOVE a maid, and fair she is,
   As fair as earth hath shown ;
I breathe no name, I tell but this—
   She lives in Worcester town.

I love a maid who's fair to view,
   A fairer none have known,
Although they've roamed earth o'er and through—
   She lives in Worcester town.

I love a maid, and fair is she,
   As fair as Heaven can own ;
And she loves me, though poor I be—
   This lass of Worcester town.

Her eyes are like the stars of night ;
   Her cheeks like rose full blown ;
Her bosom like the snowflake white—
   This lass of Worcester town.

Her voice is like the nightingale
   When sings he best in tune ;
Her breath is like spring scented vale—
   This lass of Worcester town.

This lassie fair shall bear my name ;
   And when her charms are flown,
Still will I love her all the same—
   This lass of Worcester town.

And when we both shall peaceful rest
   Beneath the churchyard stone,
Our bairns shall wish their mother blest—
   This lass of Worcester town.

VII.

WHERE Sabrina flows clear through the scene,
　　And where rises the Malvern hill blue,
Over meadows as fresh and as green
　　As a mortal on earth ever knew ;
It is there I would love to be now,
　　While sweet spring spreads her mantle so fair,
But too well doth this heart of mine know
　　That such joy cannot fall to my share.

Where Sabrina laves Berwick's wild wood,
　　In which bluebells and primroses lie,
And where Teme's (Severn's sister) clear flood
　　In one stream let their waters flow by ;
It is there I would love to be now,
　　While sweet spring spreads her mantle so fair,
But too well doth this heart of mine know
　　That such joy cannot fall to my share.

It is there that the skylark first soars,
　　When spring comes with its clear azure sky ;
It is there that his first song he pours,
　　Giving thanks that the winter's gone by ;
It is there that the nightingale's song
　　Is first heard in the coppice loud trill.
Oh ! the yearn in my bosom how strong
　　That I could as of yore be there still.

But adieu, Severn stream, cool and clear ;
　　Fond adieu, Malvern hill, high and blue ;
And farewell, Berwick wood, ever dear,
　　Where the feeling of love I first knew.
Farewell, scenes I love fondest and best,
　　I remember you though far away ;
On my heart must your images rest
　　'Till I mingle with ashes and clay.

VIII.

FROM Hallow's ford to Kempsey's bay,
    Where flows Sabrina's stream,
'Tis sweet to roam the livelong day
    When summer reigns supreme.

For clear the stream and bright the sun
    That basks himself in there,
On this wide earth stream there is none
    That flows through scene more fair.

The banks are green on which to lie
    While viewing ripples bright ;
Gay flowers, too. there greet the eye,
    And help to give delight.

At morn the lark there soars to sky
    To tell his joyous tale ;
At eve there Philomela shy
    With song fills Berwick's dale.

There blackbird dun and warbling thrush,
    With linnet, swell the strain ;
While blossom white decks hawthorn bush
    And scents wide Kempsey's plain.

If heaven on earth was ever seen
    Such sight was surely there ;
For where the spot on earth so green
    As Berwick's scene so fair ?

WHERE Sabrina flows smoothly along
　　Through the meadows of Kempsey so green;
Where the lark soars above with his song,
　And sweet flowers make pleasant the scene;
It was there that I first learnt to love,
　And first felt its warm flame in my breast;
'Twas in Kempsey's secluded cool grove
　The first vow by my tongue was exprest.

Ah, how fair was the maid I then knew,
　Even Fanny, so dear unto me,
With her cheeks like the roses in hue,
　And her lips as no cherry could be;
Oh, how white was her then spotless breast,
　And how guileless that white bosom, too;
Then, what rapture to feel my own press'd
　To the one I lov'd fondly and true!

We have bidden adieu long ago,
　And we meet in that sweet grove no more,
For another now owns the warm glow
　Of her bosom, as I did of yore;
But I know she can never forget
　The fond heart she once lov'd, and so well,
Even now, p'rhaps, her heart feels regret
　That she let her own tongue say " Farewell."

X.

ON the banks of the Severn so smooth and so
        clear,
O'er the meadows of Berwick so green,
Oh, how much would I give just to ramble now there
    To enjoy in this autumn the scene.

For how cool Kempsey's grove, and the breezes how sweet
    That blow soft from the river so near !
And the songs of the songsters how welcome their greet
    As they warble their matins so clear.

Although dead now, the flowers that bloomed there in
        spring,
    Though less green the grass may be in hue,
Still the glad birds are there that the springtime made sing,
    Nor till winter will they bid adieu.

Even now perhaps the lark may be soaring on high,
    With his carol so cheerful and glad ;
Even now as I speak Philomela may sigh
    In Ketch coppice her lay sweet and sad.

And, if so, oh, the rapture for my ears to hear
    That lark's song, or that nightingale's lay ;
For the first lark I ever heard sing soared from there,
    The first nightingale, too, I may say.

Other scenes may be green, other scenes may be fair,
    Other scenes may look pleasant to view,
But however far distant I ramble from there,
    I still yearn for the scenes I first knew.

XI.

I ROAMED these meadows oft of yore
    With Fanny, dear to me :
We heard the lark his carol pour,
    His carol glad and free.
We had no sorrow—all was joy,
    As we gaz'd on the scene ;
The sun shone brightly in the sky
    And o'er the meadows green.

I roam these meadows once again—
    The meads I oft roam'd o'er ;
I hear the lark pour out his strain
    E'en as he did of yore.
The sun shines bright in azure sky,
    The meads are green in hue :
But now my bosom heaves deep sigh-
    Fanny hath bid adieu.

THE bonniest lad in Worcester town
    Was Will of Severn side ;
The fairest lass in Worcester known
    Was Clara, Worcester's pride.
She lov'd Will for his honest heart,
    He lov'd her for her grace ;
In Christendom no youth as smart,
    Than hers no fairer face.

The cruel war broke out in Spain,
    And gallant Will was gone ;
While Clara's tear-drops fell like rain,
    And beat her fond heart lone.
He cheer'd her much with promise bright
    Ere he left Worcester town ;
For her, he said, he went to fight
    To win wealth and renown.

The fight rag'd fierce in sunny Spain,
    The carnage it was great ;
And Will was number'd with the slain,
    But bravely met his fate.
They buried him with thousands more
    Upon the open plain,
And soon the bitter war was o'er
    In bright and sunny Spain.

Miles far away, near Worcester town,
    There is a churchyard green ;
And in that churchyard is a stone
    That was not always seen.
Beneath that stone lies maiden fair,
    E'en Clara, fair and gay ;
Her heart could not the sorrow bear,
    It broke for him away.

XIII.

THE sweet spring threw her mantle green
　　Where Severn's gliding stream is seen,
Which brightly sparkled on its way,
But I, alas, was far away.

The sweet spring threw her mantle fair
Where Malvern cleaves the azure air,
While Newland's trees wore white array,
But I, alas, was far away.

The primrose bloomed in Perry's wood,
The bluebell, too, near Severn's flood ;
The violets sweet in Berwick lay,
But I, alas, was far away.

The cowslip waved on Kempsey's plain
Beside the daisy once again,
And children plucked their posies gay,
But I, alas, was far away.

The skylark rose from Teme's green banks,
And soared to heaven to render thanks,
While others listened to his lay,
But I, alas, was far away.

Once more the blackbird whistled sweet
In Kempsey's grove and cool retreat.
And piped the throstle on the may,
But I, alas, was far away.

In Pixham's green and shady grove
Sweet Philomela sang her love
When day was spent in twilight's ray,
But I, alas, was far away.

Thus spring hath come and vanished, too,
Since those sweet scenes I bade adieu,
But not with me doth rest the blame,
My heart still lingers there the same.

XIV.

I'M far away from scenes I love,
    Yet what is that to me?
My thoughts still fly to Kempsey's grove
Where coos the livelong day the dove,
    Or soars the skylark free.

They let me climb up Malvern blue,
    And roam Powick's meadows green ;
They let me long-lost joys renew—
They bring me back lost friends so true,
    To roam each peaceful scene.

I bathe in Severn's crystal stream,
    Sabrina smooth and clear ;
They let me rove by gentle Teme,
I watch its ripples dance and gleam,
    Although so far from there.

What bird hath freedom sweet like me?
    The swallows won't compare.
I let my heart and thoughts be free,
With lightning speed hence do they flee
    To roam those scenes so fair.

XV.

I ROAM once more these hills so blue—
 The hills of Malvern high ;
And how fair from here is the view
 That meets a gazer's eye.
How green the meads and woods below
 That beautify each scene ;
How clear the rills that rippling flow
 Through Colwall's meadows green.

The lark that soars in Malvern's sky
 Is glad as lark can be ;
The only thing that heaves a sigh
 In all this place is me ;
And I but sigh for friends I knew
 In happy days of yore,
Who climbed with me these hills so blue
 And Colwall's meads roamed o'er.

The Seasons.

SPRING.

I.*

'TWAS but a light and gentle breeze,
　　Yet where it passed there in its train
The buds peeped forth from leafless trees,
　　And thousand flowers decked the plain.

The brooklet laughed, the grass grew green,
　　The sun shone bright on lake and sea ;
The primrose dressed each woodland scene,
　　And songsters sang to tell their glee.

The daisies dotted valley low,
　　And moss made green the mountain high ;
The hawthorn blossom, white as snow,
　　Spread fragrance wide and pleased the eye.

The modest violet, doubly sweet,
　　Grew hiding in the shady dale ;
The bluebells gave a welcome greet,
　　And buttercups dwelt in the vale.

Thus hill and dale, and wood and heath
　　Were rendered fair, and birds made sing,
And only by the passing breath
　　Of ever-welcome, pleasant spring.

* *Worcester Herald*, June 2nd, 1883.

II.*

I COME with footsteps soft and light,
    And breezes fresh and free ;
I spread my cloak o'er vale and height,
    O'er coppice, shrub, and tree.
The buds come forth and give me greet,
    Glad songsters gaily sing,
While flowers wild in garments sweet
    Salute the gentle spring.

First comes the snowdrop, white in hue,
    And then the primrose pale ;
While by its side the violet blue
    With fragrance scents the gale ;
Neat daisies dot the meadows green,
    Bright buttercups as well ;
Cowslips bedeck each rural scene,
    And bluebells dress the dell.

On hedgerow green the blushing rose
    Succeeds the hawthorn's bloom ;
The honeysuckle climbing grows
    And sheds its rich perfume.
Each hill and dale, each wood and plain,
    With gladness seems to ring ;
And songsters wild in one glad strain
    Give welcome to the spring.

* *Worcester Herald*, March 25th, 1882.

III.

'TIS spring ! I know it by the flowers fair ;
    I know it by the sky so clear and blue ;
I know it by the sweet ambrosial air,
    And by the hills and meadows' greener hue.

I know it by the primrose in the glen ;
    I know it by the violet in the dell ;
I know it by the daisy on the plain,
    By nodding bluebells that in woodlands dwell.

I know it by the lark that soars on high ;
    I know it by the linnet in the bush ;
I know it by the nightingale so shy,
    By blackbird's note, and loudly piping thrush.

I know it by the dancing, rippling rill ;
    I know it by the river smooth and clear ;
I know it by the sun-ray gilded hill,
    And by the beams which on the sea appear.

Thus smiles the earth beneath spring's pleasant reign,
    Rejoicing that dreary winter is o'er ;
From sea to rill, from mountain to the plain,
    One language tells us spring is come once more.

IV.

I HEARD the cuckoo sing,
   And when I heard his voice
   It made my heart rejoice,
For then I knew 'twas spring.

I saw the skylark soar
   Light-winged to heaven blue,
   And by his song I knew
The winter drear was o'er.

I saw the primrose pale
   Bloom by the violet blue,
   And when I saw the two
I knew spring decked the vale.

I saw the daisy neat,
   And yellow daffodil;
   I saw the dancing rill
Flow sparkling at my feet.

I saw the fragrant May
   Bloom white on hedgerow green,
   And by each lovely scene
I knew spring held her sway.

I heard the bee loud hum;
   I saw the butterfly
   On spangled wing go by;
These, too, said spring had come.

Mount, valley, hill, and dale,
   Rill, river, lake, and sea,
   Bud, leaf, and songster free—
All told the same glad tale.

V.

O ! OUT to the meadows let us go,
    Out from the smoky town ;
Out to the glens where the brooklets flow,
Out to the dells where the wild buds grow
    In beauty all their own.

Out to the woods where the wild birds sing,
    Out from the noisy street ;
Out to the glades where glad throstles ring
Their notes of joy at the new come spring,
    And blackbirds, too, give greet.

Out, out to the open boundless plain,
    Out to the mountain high,
Where breezes blow from the distant main,
And we feel it thrill thro' pulse and vein,
    Till with very joy we sigh.

VI.

COME, gentle spring, with verdant wing,
And footsteps soft and light,
With balmy breeze that robes the trees
In leaflets green and bright ;
Come, spring, again with smiling plain,
And gushing, sparkling rill,
With daisy neat, and primrose sweet,
And violet sweeter still.

Hail, gentle spring ! Hark how birds sing
Their merry tuneful lays !
See, in the sky, the sun how high,
And how bright are his rays !
All earth seems glad, that late was sad
Beneath cold winter's reign ;
Now, all is joy, without alloy,
Since spring is come again !

DOWN by the river clear !
　　Far in the meadow green,
Where thousand flow'rets rear
　　Their heads to deck the scene !
Up on the mountain high !
　　Down in the valley low,
From whence lark soars to sky
　　His song of joy to flow !

Deep in the shady dale !
　　Out on the open plain !
In meadow, copse, and vale,
　　We see sweet spring again !
Hark, how the birds rejoice
　　With song so glad and free !
And shall not man give voice
　　To swell the jubilee ?

VIII.

ONCE more the meads look fresh and green ;
    Once more the sky looks clear and blue ;
Once more how fair is every scene
    Which in the winter bare we knew.

On sloping banks sweet violets grow,
    In shady grove blooms primrose fair ;
And hawthorn blossom, white as snow,
    With sweetest fragrance scents the air.

The buttercup and daisy neat
    Now ornament each verdant mead ;
The cowslip, with its odour sweet,
    Among them shows its yellow head.

The murm'ring brook meanders on
    Through many fair and shady ways,
Or wide expanse, where beaming sun
    In thousand dancing ripples plays.

The birds are silent now no more,
    As they were in the winter long ;
Hark ! at the lark as he doth soar,
    How gaily carols he his song.

Hark ! at the throstle, blackbird too,
    And nightingale, how sweet they sing ;
How gladly winter's bade adieu,
    How joyfully is welcomed spring.

IX.

ONCE more returns the genial spring,
   With breezes fresh, and scenes so fair ;
When happy birds their matins sing,
   And earth seems not to own a care.

The lark soars high on pinions strong,
   And carols forth his notes so gay ;
The thrush pipes loud his tuneful song,
   And Philomela gives her lay.

Once more the primrose decks the glade,
   And bluebells nod in lowly dale ;
Once more, deep in the woodland shade,
   The violet blooms and scents the vale.

Once more the daisy dots the plain,
   With buttercup and cowslip too ;
Once more the brooklet laughs again,
   And skies regain their long lost blue.

This earth is fair, but doubly so
   When spring-time dwells upon each scene ;
'Tis spring that bids wild flowers blow,
   And makes our hills and valleys green.

WINTER.

I.

ON pinions fleet sweet summer flies ;
    The blue forsakes the azure sky ;
  The leaves fall thick and lifeless lie,
And o'er the land the cold breeze sighs.

The thrush has ceased his happy song ;
  The nightingale has hushed her love ;
  The lark no more soars high above
To carol matin glad and strong.

The flowers, too, with all their pride,
  That made each scene so fresh and fair,
  That made each breeze such fragrance bear,
With summer's flight have meekly died.

The robin dons his crimson vest,
  His plaintive song again we hear,
  That song which says, " Winter is near,
And fled the days so bright and blest."

Yet winter shall not ever last ;
  Though nature may sleep for a while,
  In turn sweet spring shall come with smile,
And make forgotten winter's blast.

II.

FARE thee well, lovely summer! sweet summer, adieu!
    With thy fulness of pleasure and light!
Who will mourn not the loss of thy fathomless blue,
    And thy sunshine unspeakably bright?

Chill the breezes now blow o'er the still verdant vales,
    And less warm are the sun's fitful rays;
While the flowers quickly fade in their once sunny dales,
    And less gladly the birds trill their lays.

See! the swallows they gather together and skim
    In flocks through the air far away;
For their home cannot be where the sun groweth dim,
    But where summer supreme rules the day.

Oh, that I, like the swallows, could follow in flight
    In thy pathway, so happy and free!
Like them would I bask all my life in thy light,
    For where summer reigns, there would I be.

III.

SUMMER departs, already chill the breeze
    That sadly sighs o'er valley and o'er hill;
Thick lie the leaves beneath the half bare trees,
    Or speed them swift upon the swollen rill.

The sluggard sun no longer rises bright
    At early morn, as he was wont to do;
Nor soars the lark on pinions strong and light,
    To give him greet with matin, glad and true.

The buds are dead that made the meadows fair,
    The cowslip and the daisy bloom no more;
No violets sweet now fragrant make the air,
    Nor roses cluster round the cottage door.

The songsters, too, have ended all their lays,
    Now sad and silent is each once glad dale;
No blackbird, thrush, or linnet sing their praise,
    Nor in the coppice warbles nightingale.

The swallow leaves us for his distant home,
    The robin dons his winter crimson vest;
Loud howls the wind while brooklets race and foam,
    And dull skies tell us fled is summer blest.

Yet, let it fly, tho' winter may seem long,
    Still in its turn it, too, must pass away;
And once again all earth will team with song,
    And gladly smile 'neath spring-time's bright array.

IV.

THE wintry winds blow cold and chill;
    The trees stretch out their branches bare;
Thick mists enshroud each lofty hill,
    And beauty flies each scene once fair.

The birds that sang their songs of joy
    Are silent now, or flown away
To regions where, without alloy,
    The summer reigns the livelong day.

The countless flowers, fair and sweet,
    That made so gay our valleys green,
No longer blossom at our feet
    To brighten up the rural scene.

The rill that tinkled in the sun
    No longer courts the shady tree;
With raging voice it rushes on,
    And hurries, swollen, to the sea.

Yet wherefore all this change so sad?
    Why does not summer always reign,
And make the feathered songsters glad,
    And flowers ever deck the plain?

Oh! learn that winter does not kill—
    It only bids them sleep awhile—
For birds' sweet notes again shall trill,
    And earth look fair 'neath spring's bright smile.

Love Songs.

I.

CUPID sat by a gate with his arrows and bow,
  While his looks showed him on mischief bent ;
" Now the first who pass here, be they mighty or low,
  They shall prove why these weapons were sent.
Be they rich, be they poor, be they aged or young,
  Of my prowess their bosoms shall know,
For no mortal e'er yet was sufficiently strong
  To withstand the swift dart from my bow."

Now the first who came by was the squire so gay,
  With his heart beating free as the sea ;
Ne'er a pang had he felt, for he scorned Cupid's sway,
  Though with many a maid flirted he.
But the arrow was sped, and it entered his heart,
  And his freedom for ever was gone ;
Yet he saw not the imp who had winged the swift dart,
  For that instant young Cupid had flown.

Now the next who passed by was a poor peasant lass,
  With her cheeks like two roses in June,
While her eyes not the summer's bright sun could surpass,
  Or her voice not the skylark in tune.
But the arrow was sped, and it entered her breast,
  And her freedom for ever was gone.
She may try, 'tis in vain, she will never know rest
  Till the gallant who stole it is won.

" Tell me not," said the youth, " that my station is high ;
  Tell me not that your own is too low ;
All the wealth in this world would not save me a sigh,
  Or give bliss which with you I should know.
Though my wealth may be great, I can share it with you,
  With my station your charms will combine ;
There is nothing can part two fond hearts loving true ;
  I am yours, if you will but be mine."

To J.

II.

WHEN the dawn beameth grey in the cold eastern
    sky,
  And the breeze cometh fresh o'er the lea,
While the song of the lark is heard ringing on high,
  It is then that I think upon thee.

When the twilight gloams soft in calm eve's gentle hour,
  And all nature at rest seems to be,
It is then I am lost in sweet memory's power,
  It is then that I think upon thee.

When the stars twinkle bright in the clear sky above,
  And the moon sails aloft high and free,
It is then in sweet sleep that I dream of my love,
  It is then that I dream, dear, of thee.

III.

To W. H.

I HAVE seen maid with lip as red
   As cherry with its brilliant hue ;
Yet, maid, believe the word now said—
   The reddest lip belongs to you.

I have seen maid with cheek as smooth
   As ever marble's surface knew ;
Yet, maid, believe I speak the truth—
   The smoothest cheek is own'd by you.

I have seen maid with eye as bright
   As summer's sun in sky of blue ;
Yet, maid, believe my tongue speaks right—
   The brightest eye is own'd by you.

I have seen maid with breast as white
   As ever snow was to the view ;
But snow ne'er cover'd mountain's height
   So white as bosom own'd by you.

Give me that lip, give me that cheek,
   The beaming eye, that bosom, too,
And true shall be the vow I speak,
   Which is, that I will love but you.

To F.

IV.

WHEN leaf and thorn with dew of morn
　　Like diamond glisten bright,
And in the sky the lark soars high
　　On wings so free and light,
How sweet the scene, so fresh and green,
　　How pleasant mead and grove ;
But more so when I roam the glen
　　With her I most do love.

When falls moon's beam on crystal stream,
　　Or dances on the rill ;
When stars so bright rise on the night
　　And sink behind the hill ;
When through the trees blows gentle breeze,
　　Or whispers through the grove,
Oh, then what bliss to feel the kiss
　　From lips of her I love.

V.*

SHE sat upon the shore alone,
  And gazed across the sea ;
The ship that held her swain was gone
  To a land he said was free.
Her tears fell fast, and deep the sighs
  Which rose from her white breast.
" Will he return," were all her cries,
  " And make me once more blest ? "

Her lover found the land he sought,
  And wealth and riches came ;
And now the time had come, he thought,
  He would the maiden claim.
He crossed the sea to England's shore,
  With heart both light and gay ;
He sought the maid he loved of yore,
  To name the bridal day.

" Where is the maiden fair I knew ? "
  In accents wild he cried ;
The words they answered him were few—
  " Years long ago she died."
They took him to the churchyard green,
  And showed him where she lay ;
For him her heart had faithful been,
  It broke that parting day.

---

* *Worcester Herald*, November 24th, 1883.

c

VI.

To F. G.

I CHANC'D to look an album through,
    And in the book I saw the face
Of one whom years ago I knew,
    Whose image still my heart bears trace.

Smooth was the cheek and bright the eye
    Of her upon whose face I gaz'd ;
And as of yore I heav'd a sigh
    To think how vain my love had blaz'd.

But she heard not the deep drawn-sighs
    I heav'd of yore, and still heave now ;
Our path in life too distant lies
    For her, my love, to ever know.

In silence, then, my love shall rest,
    As it hath rested in the past ;
But while with life I am possess'd
    The flame will still as fervent last.

VII.

To J. K.

I KNOW a maiden fair,
　A maiden far away;
She is my guiding star,
　And dear to me the ray.
I dream of her by night,
　And think of her by day;
Thus ever in my sight
　Is she, though far away.

Her eyes are like the pips
　Which lie in ripest pear;
Like cherries are her lips—
　Their kisses, oh! how dear!
Her cheeks are like the rose
　That blooms in month of May;
Her bosom whiter glows
　Than snow in winter's day.

This maid I prize the best
　Of all maids known to me;
More dear than all the rest
　Were, or can ever be.
One wish alone is mine,—
　That I as dear may be,
For then our love will twine
　As ivy to the tree.

VIII.

To F.

IF days were happy, now gone past,
　When thou didst but me *see*,
What will they be when these are pass'd,
　And I *belong* to thee ?

Then will I try with all my heart
　To gladden that of thine ;
Nor shall my love for thee depart
　And give thee cause to pine.

Then quick shall fade each pang and throe
　Which thou through me hast felt,
And every sorrow thou dost know
　In sweetest bliss shall melt.

IX.

To Miss W.

IS it in smile to prove what joy
  Doth dwell within a mortal's breast?
Is it, dear maid, in deep-drawn sigh
  To make a bosom's grief express'd?
If so, what joy then must be thine,
  Since smiles for ever rest with thee?
If so, what sorrow must be mine,
  Since sighs do ever dwell with me?

Is it in brightness of an eye
  To prove what is a bosom's weal?
Is it in teardrop, or in sigh,
  To prove what lonely breast may feel?
If so, then happy is the heart
  Within thy bosom pure and white;
If so, then mine must own a smart,
  Nor know, like thine, what is delight.

Still thine the pow'r, my dearest maid,
  To make our bosoms equal be;
For, say the word, my grief will fade,
  And I shall be as glad as thee;
My eye as bright, my heart as light,
  As eye of thine, and heart in thee,
And every sorrow take its flight,
  If thou wilt say thou " lovest me."

X.

To ANNIE.

I CAME with heart both light and glad,
  I came with bosom free ;
I leave thee with a bosom sad,
  As sad as breast can be.
I came with thrilling sense of joy—
  A stranger unto pain ;
But now, oh ! deeply do I sigh,
  And sorrow fills each vein.

I knew but joy, I felt but bliss,
  When first I came to thee ;
Now every joy is gone amiss
  Since thou wast known to me.
And, in return, what have I won
  For heart and true love given ?
Why, sorrows many, pleasures none,
  And hell made of a heaven.

XI.

DECEITFUL TOM.

A FAIRER maid was never seen,
     Nor jollier fellow either,
Than Moseley's pride, sweet Bessie Green,
And Tom, her gallant lover.

Her eyes were dark as starless night,
     His were the hue of azure;
Her bosom matched the snowflake white,
And his was her best treasure.

The morning came when they should wed,
     And lovely was the weather,
But ere that lovely day had fled
     It prov'd him a deceiver;

For false Tom lov'd another maid,
     And told the same to either;
Both maids believ'd the vows he said,
     But, ah! he married neither.

The morning came, but Tom was gone,
     And gone no one knew whither.
Who thought such thing he could have done—
     Could prove such base deceiver?

XII.

To ANNIE W.

WHAT dreary months have passed me by
    Since you and I together met ;
How often has my breast heaved sigh,
    And absence filled me with regret.
How often I have thought on you,
    And wished your form was only near ;
For yours the fault I bid adieu,
    Because I found I was not dear.

Long months have fled, and will again,
    Ere you and I, dear maid, can meet ;
Yet in the midst of ache and pain
    My heart less fond hath never beat ;
It hath, alas ! but fonder grown,
    As absence will make all hearts true ;
That yours for mine such love could own
    Who then so happy as we two ?

XIII.

To K. S.

THE rose is fair that June doth blow,
　　Its hue no flower can surpass;
Yet there is cheek of maid I know
　　That's fairer still—'tis thine, dear lass.

The ray is bright that lightly gleams
　　From summer's sun thro' azure sky;
But brighter far the ray that beams
　　From eye of maiden fair and shy.

The snow is white that winter gives
　　To cover nature's naked plain;
But whiter still that breast which heaves
　　With love, nor yet feels love in vain.

The cheek so fair, the eye so bright,
　　The bosom matchless in its hue,
Shall be to me life's one delight,
　　For she who owns them I love true.

To B.

SOME love an eye that beameth blue,
   And boast how bright its rays ;
Some love an eye with hazel hue,
   And give it best of praise ;
But give to me a darker shade,
   An eye which black doth shine ;
Nor deem I flatter thee, dear maid,
   To say, " an eye like thine."

An eye of blue may have its charm,
   The hazel one the same ;
But neither will strike *love's* alarm
   Like eye with hue I name.
Let those prize blue who love such true,
   Let those for brown choose free ;
Let some prize, too, a lighter hue,
   But an eye that's dark for me.

XV.

To W.

SWEET was the kiss I had to-day,
 The kiss, dear maid, thou gavest me ;
No wonder that my heart beat gay
 When I received the gift from thee.

Honey is sweet, I've heard it said,
 As sweet as any thing can be ;
And yet, believe me, dearest maid,
 'Tis not so sweet as kiss from thee.

They say, too, that sweet is the dew
 Which on the roses fair we see ;
And yet, dear maid, believe me true,
 'Tis not so sweet as kiss from thee.

As loves the bee to stay and sip
 The dew from every flower free,
So would I love to press thy lip,
 Nor leave while there was kiss for me.

XVI.

To MARIA.

FAIR maiden, sing that song again,
　　It cheers my sorrowed heart ;
My ear ne'er heard so sweet a strain
　　From mortal's lips depart ;
It filled my heart, it thrilled my soul,
　　With bliss I cannot name ;
It made me lose my heart's control
　　In love's all-scorching flame.

Oh ! sing that song again, dear maid,
　　And I will list to thee ;
Nor shall remembrance of it fade
　　While memory dwells in me.
Thy notes have struck a tender chord
　　That death alone can still ;
Maid, let that song once more be heard,
　　And my one wish fulfil.

XVII.

To A. W.

I SING my songs not with the strain
    I sang them long ago ;
That strain I shall not sing again,
    For dead is love's fond glow.

I sing my songs not with the tone
    I sang them once of yore,
For that which thrilled the song is gone,
    And love can come no more.

To MAGGIE.

EACH time I gaze upon your face
    What wishes fill my breast—
That I might feel your warm embrace,
    And be unto you press'd.

Yet if such pleasure could be given
    I still the same should sigh,
For life would seem too much a heaven,
    And all too quick would fly.

XVIII.

To F.

WHERE Severn's stream doth glide
    Through Kempsey's shady grove,
Where violets meekly hide
    From those who there may rove;
'Tis even near this spot,
    Where coos the turtle dove,
That can be seen the cot
    Where lives the maid I love.

Where Severn gently flows
    Through Kempsey's banks so green,
Where tansey and wild rose
    Make sweeter look the scene;
'Tis even near this spot,
    Where soars the lark above,
That can be seen the cot
    Where lives the maid I love.

Her eyes are far more blue
    Than violets in the dale;
Her breast hath whiter hue
    Than snow in winter's gale;
Her voice hath sweeter tone
    Than skylark glad and free;
Such is the maid I own—
    Sweet F., so dear to me.

XIX.

To A. W.

THE bright moon climbs the evening sky,
    The stars shine clear and bright ;
My bosom fond heaves many a sigh
    To bid my love " good-night."

The moon sails through the still night sky,
    The stars shine bright above,
And slumber sweet weighs down mine eye :—
    I dream of her I love.

The moon hath sunk in western sky,
    The stars have paled their rays ;
The sun in eastern sky rides high :—
    I wake, my love to praise.

XX.

To P.

'TIS sweet to sit beside a stream
   On spring or summer days
And see it sparkle with the beam
   That on each ripple plays;
'Tis sweet to sit beside a rill
   And hear it murmur by,
But how much sweeter is the thrill
   When one we love is nigh.

'Tis sweet to sit in shady wood
   When leaves are green in spring
And hear the glad birds warble loud
   And songs of rapture sing;
'Tis sweet to sit in silent glade
   And breathe its balmy air,
But doubly sweet when youth and maid
   The joy together share.

XXI.

To A.

WHEN I wander alone o'er this world far and wide,
  And I cross the deep ocean so blue,
I shall wish for a form to be near to my side,
  And the form that I mean, dear, is you.

Oh! we part, and perchance we shall meet not again,
  Yea, for ever may prove that adieu ;
But the pang that inflicts on my bosom most pain
  Is to feel I am loved not by you.

If I were, do you think you could tarry behind ?
  To my side would you not hasten true ?
And together face summer's or winter's cold clime,
  Nor feel pang so I was but with you.

D

XXII.

To E. G.

SOME hearts love gold, and hoard their wealth,
  And some more value fame ;
While wiser ones prize most sweet health
  Than wealth or endless name ;
But I know what is dearer far
  Than either of the three :
It is to feel my bosom share
  The joys of love with thee.

One smile from thee I value more
  Than all the wealth of earth.
What charm is there in gilded ore
  Compared with Cupid's mirth ?
What is there in an endless name,
  Or yet in health so sweet,
If blest not with love's happy flame,
  And stranger to its greet ?

Not all the wealth on earth, in sea,
  However much it be,
Could match the pleasure felt by me
  In winning *love* from thee ;
And health so sweet, and endless name,
  Would also as nought be,
At least, compared with love's fond flame,
  To kiss and clasp from thee.

XXIII.

To THE MAID I LOVE.

THE maid I love is fair to view :
  Her eyes are bright,
  Her bosom white,
Her cheeks like rose in hue.

Her teeth are like the flakes of snow ;
  But lips as red
  As coral bed,
Or cherries' crimson glow.

But, oh ! how cold that bosom is !
  For 'tis her joy
  To hear me sigh
And hold from me all bliss.

I wish her bosom soft and white
  Would let depart
  To me its heart ;
Oh ! this would be delight.

I then should deem that heaven was won ;
  Nor on earth aught
  More could be sought,
While happier would be none.

XXIV.

To A. W.

THE spring, dear maid, is fresh and green ;
  The birds pour forth their songs of joy,
To see so fair each lovely scene,
  Nor 'midst their joys feel one alloy ;
Yet how soon spring doth take its flight,
  With all its freshness glad and sweet ;
Still who can mourn, since summer bright
  Comes smiling in with rosy feet ?

Oh ! bright is summer, and its skies
  How clear, how lovely, and how blue ;
How sweet the fragrance which doth rise
  From hill and meadow fair to view ;
And yet how soon doth summer fly,
  And follow in the steps of spring ;
Still few do mourn when 'tis gone by,
  For flowers bloom and birds still sing.

Then autumn with full plenty comes,
  And welcome, too, her proffered store ;
Luxuriant mead where bee loud hums,
  And trees with luscious fruit crowned o'er.
But quickly is the autumn sped,
  And takes, like spring and summer, flight ;
Then may some hearts in silence dread
  Cold winter's long and darkened night.

Yet even winter flies at last
  With all its dreariness and pain ;
Forgotten is the bitter blast,
  And gentle spring comes back again.
Thus change the seasons' clime and hue,
  And will as long as time shall be ;
But ne'er shall change the heart so true
  Which beats within my breast for thee.

XXV.

To ——.

WHEN softly breaks the dawn of day
O'er mountain peak so high and free,
And from low mead soars skylark gay,
'Tis then I think, dear maid, of thee !

When rides the sun in sky of blue,
And dances on each rill and sea,
'Tis then I think of one loved true,
'Tis then I think, dear maid, of thee !

When sinks the sun in crimson west,
And shadows lengthen 'neath each tree,
While warbling songsters seek the nest,
'Tis then I think, dear maid, of thee !

When twilight comes so soft and sweet,
And calmness dwells on hill and lea,
'Tis then my heart doth fonder beat,
Yes, fonder beats, dear maid, for thee !

When sails the moon through skies of night,
And twinkling stars in heaven we see,
I roam beneath the flood of light,
And while I roam I think of thee !

Oh, gentle maid, believe me true,
Thou art the dearest unto me ;
Such love as mine none ever knew ;
No maid was ever lov'd like thee !

XXVI.

To P. L.

YOU ask me why some hearts are sad;
    I'll tell you if you choose;
Though yours I know is ever glad,
    Nor does one joy refuse.
A rosy cheek, a laughing eye,
    Speak well the bliss you own;
Your bosom white ne'er heaves a sigh
    To say *your* heart is lone.

I'll tell you why some hearts are sad,
    For well the cause I know,
Since joyless heart long I have had,
    And all through love's warm glow.
It makes hearts sad to love in vain
    And find each fond hope fly;
It makes hearts sad to be kept twain
    From those for whom they sigh.

And mine is sad e'er since the day
    I met you but to part,
For I alone felt love's strong sway
    Fall on my then free heart;
And yet you ask me why some hearts
    Are ever sad and lone,
When 'tis your joy to deal the smarts
    Which make that sadness known.

XXVII.

To L. H.

I KNOW maiden most fair who hath eye beaming bright,
  Even bright as an eye of a mortal can be ;
I know maiden most fair with a heart beating light,
  And the heart of that maid I know beateth for me.

I know maiden most fair with a cheek like the rose,
  And with lips like the coral so deep in the sea ;
Yet how sweet those lips are only one mortal knows,
  For those lips print their kisses alone upon me.

I know maiden most fair with a bosom like snow,
  And within that white bosom a heart warm and free ;
So my own for that bosom for ever shall glow,
  For I know that its love is but given to me.

Need I say, Lizzie dear, who the fair maiden is ?
  Need I say, Lizzie dear, who that maiden must be ?
If so, then give heed, for I utter only this—
  The fair maiden I mean is no other than thee.

XXVIII.

To FANCY.

COME, maid, with me to where rills flow
    Through meadows green and fair,
And to the grove where bluebells grow,
    And violets scent the air ;
Come, maid, with me where daisy neat
    With buttercup doth dwell,
And there I'll bask me at your feet,
    And love's devotion tell.

We'll watch the lark soar up on high,
    And hear his song of bliss ;
While, should my bosom heave a sigh,
    May it be killed with kiss ;
And as the bee sips from each flower,
    So will I sip from thee,
And sigh at each departing hour
    Which flies o'er thee and me.

XXIX.

To A. W.

WHEN beams the sun at early morn,
    Making night's gloom and darkness flee,
Showing the dewdrop on the thorn,
    'Tis then, dear maid, I think of thee.

When high the sun rides in the sky,
    And carols loud the skylark free
O'er meadows pleasant to the eye,
    'Tis then, dear maid, I think of thee.

When twilight calm, soft, and serene,
    Steals gently over land and sea,
And pensive seems each fading scene,
    'Tis then, dear maid, I think of thee.

When night, with mantle dark and drear,
    Hides all, and earth dead seems to be,
'Tis then I dream of one most dear,
    'Tis then, dear maid, I dream of thee.

XXX.

To F. A.

I'M married now, and so is she
   I loved and held so dear.
I wonder if she thinks of me
   As I oft do of her.
I wonder if she ever sighs
   To think we loved in vain;
Or if hot tears e'er dim her eyes
   That we are now in twain.

I only viewed a spot to-day
   Where we once sat of yore,
And once again love proved his sway
   Stronger than e'er before;
It brought me back those olden days
   When life had not a pain;
Oh, that I could bask in her rays,
   And live those days again.

XXXI.

To Miss C.

WHY should an eye tho' black as night
  Make faster throb another's heart?
Why should a breast tho' snowy white
  Make *love* within another start?
Is there such power in a ray
  Which beameth from a maiden's eye?
Is there in breast so strong a sway
  That it can make another sigh?

There is; for when those eyes met mine
  How soon my heart its freedom lost;
And when I saw that breast of thine,
  How many sighs the seeing cost.
How doubly quick my heart did beat,
  How doubly hot my blood did glow,
To meet the rays of eyes so sweet,
  And view the breast more white than snow.

Deem not I flatter thee, dear maid,
  To give such praise as I have done.
Is night as black as thine eyes' shade?
  Or is as bright the summer's sun?
Is winter's snow so white in hue
  As that same bosom owned by thee?
Whoever sees it must love true,
  Tho' none shall love as true as me.

XXXII.

To E. W.

IT must have been a dream I dreamed
    That I was loved by thee ;
A thought my bosom must have deemed,
    But which true could not be.

It must have been a dream of mine
    That I was dear to thee ;
That once my heart was dear to thine,
    As thine is dear to me.

I must have dreamed that I once roved
    In rapture by thy side ;
Dreamed that I was once much beloved,
    And nought to me denied.

I must have dreamed, in slumber sweet,
    That I was once most dear ;
That oft in kiss our lips did meet,
    My ears fond vows did hear.

It must have been a dream I know—
    A dream that was untrue,
Else could thy breast so cease to glow,
    Or bid this cold adieu ?

XXXIII.

To E. S. W.

SPRING lasts but for a time,
  The same with summer, too,
And autumn's golden prime
  In winter bids adieu.
The seasons come and go
  Like visions in a dream ;
Spring's green and winter's snow
  Alike on Time's swift stream.

As fled the fleeting spring,
  As fled the summer bright,
As autumn, too, took wing,
  With winter in its flight,
So changed thy heart to me
  Which loved me once so well,
Yet never I to thee
  Will change while here I dwell.

Springs green shall come and go,
  Bright summers, too, shall fly,
And many an autumn's glow
  Shall fade in winter's sky ;
But these shall never see
  Less constant burn this flame ;
Unchanged I am to thee,
  And e'er shall be the same.

XXXIV.

To Miss B.

A TONGUE, dear maid, may silent be,
    An eye may show indiff'rent ray,
(E'en as mine did when I passed thee,)
    Yet bosom feel love's potent sway.

For how much quicker my heart beat
    When thy form came so near to mine;
How much I sighed to bid no greet,
    Since stranger my form was to thine.

How blessed is he who knows thee well,
    And feels his hand in thine own pressed;
But happier he who hears thee tell
    Thy heart is his to make him blessed.

I wish I were but either one—
    The latter one I should think best—
Of sorrow then I should feel none,
    And joy with me would ever rest.

XXXV.

To CLARA.

I HAVE sighed, Clara dear, since you bade me adieu ;
    I shall sigh till you meet me again ;
But I wonder the while if your bosom sighs too,
    And, like mine, feels of grief and of pain.
I have sighed, Clara dear, since you bade me farewell ;
    I shall sigh till you meet me again ;
And how soon shall that greeting my anguish dispel,
    And make sorrow come near me in vain.

It is sweet to be near to the one whom we love,
    It is sad from them parted to be ;
But perchance neither parting nor meeting doth prove
    Half so much unto you as to me ;
If it doth, then how much is your grief and your woe
    When you wish me farewell and adieu ;
But how much more the joy that your bosom shall know
    When fond meeting restores me to you.

XXXVI.

To A. W.

THE rose I had from thee is dead,
  Its colour faded, odour fled,
    And all its freshness gone ;
'Twould make one think, to see it now,
Sweet bloom its leaves did never know,
    For beauty it hath none.

Yet once how charming and how fair,
How much of beauty was its share
    When it was giv'n to me ;
How fresh and rich its lovely bloom.
How fragrant was its sweet perfume ;
    'Twas fair as rose could be.

It nearly matched the blushing cheek
Of her who gave it, pure and meek—
    The maid I love so well ;
And that's enough to prove its worth,
For fairer maid is not on earth,
    My tongue can truly tell.

'Tis faded now, and yet how dear
It doth unto my eyes appear,
    The same as when first giv'n ;
And it shall be by me possessed
While on this earth in life I rest,
    And then, perhaps, in heav'n.

XXXVII.

To CLARA.

L IKE two rivers which start from one fountain,
     Getting wider as each flows its way;
Like two ranges which part from one mountain,
     And in branching get wider astray;
Like two ripples which start from one billow,
     And in ocean get wider apart;
As in emblem dog-rose is to willow,
     So to me, dearest Clara, thou art.

I have tried—yet how vain the endeavour—
     To make fonder thy heart unto mine;
But the more thou hast made us to sever,
     And kept still in the path that was thine.
I have offered thee love the sincerest
     That a mortal's fond bosom could feel,
Yet that love thou hast never held dearest,
     But hath met it with bosom of steel.

Do not blame me if e'er my heart seeketh
     A fond maid who shall love me more true;
Do not blame me if time ever wreaketh
     On your bosom a pang as mine knew.
If we knock and the door will not open,
     From that heart how soon turn we away,
And seek other that gladly will soften,
     And rejoice to be bound in love's sway.

XXXVIII.

To S.

ALTHO' many may wish thee much joy on this day
    In a language more tender than mine,
Yet no heart wishes more, my tongue truly can say,
    Than this one of mine wishes for thine.

May this day come to thee, dearest friend of my heart,
    Without sorrow, or pain, or a throe ;
May this day see from thee every grief depart,
    If such thing thy white bosom can know.

May this day bring to thee nought but gladness and joy,
    Even such as feel angels in heaven,
While each one that ensues thy bliss never alloy,
    Nor with anguish thy bosom make riven.

And as birthdays succeed, and thy youth takes its flight,
    May thy friends still increase and be true ;
But whoever may rove, or inconstant may prove,
    Know my friendship will bid no adieu.

XXXIX.

To Miss FRANKLYN.

WHY did my heart so quickly beat
When thou and I first met?
Why such joy felt at the first greet?
At parting such regret?
Why in long absence have I thought
Ever the most of thee?
And 'mongst earth's thousands thy form sought
As dearest unto me?

'Tis years ago since first we met
As strangers only do;
The years flew by;—did I forget
The face and form I knew?
Aye, many others I have known
Whose forms were fair to see;
Yet, maid, believe me, thou alone
Wast dearest unto me.

We're met again, and 'tis for thee
To say if we meet more;
I still can say the love thrills me
Which I felt once of yore;
And while doth beat this heart of mine
That love must dwell there too;
The dearest heart on earth is thine,
In meet or in adieu.

XL.

To ——.

THERE is a thrill no tongue can tell—
   So warm, so hot its glow ;
There is a flame tongue cannot name
   Which but few bosoms know.
There is a zeal some hearts do feel,
   But, oh ! how few are they,
And when once felt how soon will melt
   All else within its sway.

I know one heart which feels this part,
   Altho' so much it be ;
I know a heart which would impart
   This feeling unto thee.
For thee it is I feel all this,
   Although 'tis felt in vain ;
For well I know no heart hast thou
   To give to me again.

XLI.

To EMILY W.

THE words, though simple in their form,
　　That issued through thy lips so red,
Have made again my heart beat warm,
　　And raised bright hopes I thought were dead.

The thought that I might be forgot
　　Had nearly drowned my hopes with grief ;
But thy sweet words have cheered my lot,
　　And given my lonely heart relief.

As dew falls on the arid plain,
　　So fell those words upon my ear ;
But I should try to tell in vain
　　How much I hold that whisper dear.

XLII.

To PATTIE L.

I HAVE travelled, maid, many a mile,
    Over land, and the same over sea,
I have met, dear, with many a smile
    From fair maidens, as fair as could be,
I have kissed many a lip that was red,
    Even redder than cherry could be,
But the best kiss my lips ever had
    Was the kiss that was given me by thee.

Tho' we met but as strangers do meet,
    Yet we parted not strangers the same,
For how soon didst thou give me warm greet,
    And thy smiles put my heart in a flame ;
And what rapture I felt in each kiss
    That thy lips pressed so oft unto me !
Whose the tongue that can tell half the bliss
    That I felt at such favours from thee ?

But farewell, my dear maid, I must say,
    Fond adieu I must bid unto thee,
Though how far, how far distant the day
    When forgotten thou wilt be by me ;
When remembrance doth fade in my heart
    Of thy smiles and thy kisses so free,
It will be when I've ended life's part,
    It will be when I've ceased, maid, to be.

XLIII.

To JENNIE K.

I WRITE thee this to have on thy birthday,
  To prove it is forgotten not by me,
Although so long thou hast been far away
  From him who loves, and only loves but thee.

Mine was to-day, but no fond missive came
  To wish me happy, and to bring me joy,
A proof thy bosom doth not feel the same
  As this of mine, which for thine own doth sigh.

I fondly hoped (although such hope was vain)
  To have thy greeting when the morn came round ;
How much I sighed, for how much was my pain
  To find each hope my heart held cast aground.

Yet, though mine pass'd without a greet from thee,
  Without a wish that joy might be my own,
No need through such that thine the same should'st be,
  But rather rapture to thee should'st be known.

Such is the wish that's echoed from my heart—
  Thou to be happy on thy natal day,
And may heaven more, aye, and more joy impart
  As o'er thy head each birthday flies away.

XLIV.

To CLARA.

WHEN of yore, dearest Clara, we parted,
    And in anger were silent so long,
Do not think 'twas thine heart only smarted
    With the blow all so cruel and wrong.
For how often my bosom was sighing
    For the form I loved, fondest and true ;
And how often my wishes went flying
    To the maid I had bidden adieu.

Yet that parting hath not been for nothing,
    Though it gave both our bosoms such pain,
(Which is lost in the balm and the soothing
    Of our being united again.)
For the parting proved well that I love thee
    Of all maids on this wide earth the best ;
I feel joy when thy form is beside me,
    I feel heaven when I am to thee pressed.

XLV.

To ——.

FAIR one, wilt thou list to a tale,
  A tale that I would tell to thee ?
If so, believe it shall not fail
  To prove how dear thou art to me.

I did but gaze on thee to-night,
  I did but see thy form pass by,
That moment saw my heart take flight,
  And only, too, to fly to thee.

I feel as if not only heart
  But that my *soul* has left me, too ;
Oh ! lady fair, bid them depart,
  And seek their owner, fond and true.

And yet, unless my heart brings thine,
  It will be worthless unto me ;
E'en life itself I must resign
  Without 'tis rendered bless'd by thee.

XLVI.

To JULIA.

WEEP not, dear maid—at least for me,
　For I am gaily-hearted ;
I've oft met maids, as I meet thee,
　But from them all have parted.
I freely roam like busy bee
　On summer's flowers started ;
He sips their sweets, then away will flee—
　Like him I am free-hearted.

Weep not, dear maid—at least for me,
　For I am happy ever ;
Let only pleasure dwell with thee,
　Make sorrow from thee sever ;
For what can grieving e'er avail,
　Though I may be departed ?
It will but make those fair cheeks pale,
　And leave thee broken-hearted.

XLVII.

To Miss ——.

OH ! gentle maid, I did but gaze
  A moment on thy face,
When in my bosom burnt a blaze
  That time can not efface ;
For when my spirit wings its flight
  From all that earth hath given,
My soul with thine would fain unite,
  And live as one in heaven.

XLVIII.

To E. W.

I DID not think, my lady fair,
    That I should ever make blush rise
Upon thy cheek, like I saw there
    Last night, when met our laughing eyes.

And why that blush came o'er thy cheek
    I cannot guess, I cannot name,
Else should my tongue the reason speak,
    Although in such I might give blame.

I've heard it said that only love
    Can make a cheek to blush the same ;
But, ah ! too well I now can prove
    A blush can rise without love's flame.

I blushed as well, tho' with it, too,
    A sigh escaped this breast of mine ;
But I alone of either knew,
    Nor was it guessed by heart of thine.

Nor was the blush and deep sigh all
    I felt, dear lady, and through thee ;
Tongue cannot tell, and pen ne'er shall,
    How troubled my heart felt in me.

But more on this I must not dwell,
    For it perchance may give thee pain ;
One thing I know, and know too well,
    I love but thee, and love in vain.

XLIX.

To F. A.

WHERE the hills rise blue, and the meads lie green,
  And the Teme flows for ever clear,
How my heart would love o'er that scene to rove
  With the maiden I hold so dear.
But I know full well that such cannot be,
  For we parted long years ago,
Yet I love her still, though she loves not me,
  With a flame that few bosoms know.

I may climb those hills, roam those meadows green,
  As I did in the days gone by,
But I care not now for the lovely scene—
  It is viewed with a listless eye ;
For the one who made each sweet scene so blest
  Would not be by my side as then.
We have parted for e'er, though I love her best,
  We shall roam those sweet spots ne'er again.

L.

To Miss McK.

THERE is a thrill that all do feel
    Once in a lifetime, soon or late ;
Alike the heart and breast of steel,
    As those more fond, and more elate.

There is a thrill that all have felt
    Who've trodden life's path on this earth ;
There is a thrill that will be dealt
    To all who do own mortal birth.

That thrill, dear maid, is *Love* by name,
    Its sense is felt deep in the heart ;
And when a heart once feels this flame
    It never can be made depart.

Maid, hast thou never felt this thrill
    Pierce thy white bosom or thy heart ?
If not, I hope 'twill be fate's will
    To bid thee feel for me love's dart.

LI.

To POLLY G.

WHEN you say, " I think little of you,"
    You know not, dearest maid, what you say,
For, believe me, I'm speaking most true
    When I say, " I think of you all day ;"
And when night bids me seek peaceful rest,
    It is filled with bright visions all through,
Oh! those visions how sweet and how blest,
    For I dream, dearest maiden, of you.

Shall I say what my thoughts are by day?
    Shall I tell what my dreams are by night?
Lend your ear, if you say that I may,
    For they are all of joy and delight.
Through the day this one thought is my share,
    That my form by your own is loved best;
Whilst in dreams, dearest maiden, I dare
    In embraces of love to be pressed.

LII.

To E. H.

I KNOW a maid, and so do you,
  Who loves me more than all beside,
And who will ever live me true,
  Whatever fortune may betide.

You know a youth, and so do I,
  Who loves you, as are loved but few ;
Now, Lizzie, can you this deny—
  The one is I, the other you ?

LIII.

To Miss McK.

"HENCEFORTH as friends." How vain that word
   Which bids this tie between us glow,
For hast thou, dear maid, never heard,
   This feeling perished long ago ?
While if the feeling *did* exist,
   Would it suffice for what I sought ?
Oh ! do not think *love* could be miss'd
   And be by *friendship's* feeling bought.

"Henceforth as friends," with thee alone
   This friendship's feeling then must rest,
For, maid, I must to thee make known
   No thrill but *love* can fill this breast.
Thy heart may change, and love me not,
   I must love thee, dear maid, the same ;
Thy heart may bid me be forgot,
   But with me still must burn love's flame.

LIV.

To MAGGIE.

SWEET maid, possess'd of every charm,
    Of every charm a maid can boast,
What youth could ever do thee harm ?
    Not I, who loves thee best, and most.

I love to gaze on those bright eyes,
    In brightness brighter than sun's rays,
Although this heart of mine quite dies,
    Beneath so hot and bright a blaze.

I love to view those cheeks of thine,
    So smooth, and like the roses fair,
And wish those lips were pressed to mine,
    To taste the dew that they do bear.

I love to gaze upon thy breast,
    That bosom whiter than the snow ;
And how I wish I was possess'd
    Of all the joys it could bestow.

Oh, say thou wilt not these deny,
    But that thou wilt bestow them me.
If not, for ever I shall sigh,
    But given, how blest I then shall be.

LV.

To Mrs. B.

I HEAR thou lik'st me not,
  Come, lady, tell me why
Such feeling was begot,
  Nor do my wish deny.
Now quickly will I heed
  What thy tongue says to me,
And earn a better meed
  Than that one giv'n by thee.

Yet, strange it seems to me
  That thou, a stranger quite,
(And who such will e'er be)
  Should'st feel such at first sight.
Is it the looks I own
  That made thee feel such hate?
If so, how ugly grown
  I must have got of late.

Or, was it my low birth
  That sank me in thine eyes,
And deemed me meaner earth
  Than that which wealth supplies?
Fair lady, do not weigh
  Man's worth by what's possessed,
Like him, wealth is but clay,
  And gilded dust at best.

LVI.

To EMMA.

THE last adieu, so lately said,
    Between my form and thine,
Will never make thy bosom sad,
    Like it hath saddened mine.

With thee, adieu seemed not a death,
    Like as it seemed to me,
With thee, it seemed but so much breath,
    Forgotten, then, by thee.

I would that I were like thee, too,
    Not griev'd at love's farewell,
I then could smile at thy adieu,
    Forget thy form as well.

LVII.

To Miss B.

COLD is the snow December snows
    In winter's cheerless reign ;
Cold is the blast December blows
    O'er hill and naked plain ;
Cold is the ice keen winter sees
    On river, lake, and sea ;
Yet not so cold is one of these
    As look which came from thee.

Yet do not think I seek from thee
    A kinder, warmer ray ;
I would not have given unto me .
    What thy heart says me nay.
Preferred the look, however cold,
    If prompted by thy heart,
To smile, which would, like painter's gold,
    Be made hide meaner part.

LVIII.

To T. J. E.

TO sink in sleep and dream of thee
　　Is life's sincerest joy,
For while sweet slumber comes to me
　　'Tis then I cease to sigh.

To sink in sleep and dream of thee
　　Is all I wish to do,
For what on earth can better be
　　Than dream thou lov'st me true?

If, when the spirit takes its flight,
　　Such visions still come then,
How much I wish to sleep to-night,
　　Nor ever wake again.

LIX.

To A.

SWEET the love that owns no fear
  In its path of wooing;
Sweet the love that sheds no tear
  In the moments suing.
Cupid is a wayward thing,
  Either good or teasing;
Some he loves to deal a sting,
  To others be most pleasing.

Minnie, we have felt him both,
  As you will confess me,
Since you were once very loth
  To let favours bless me;
Then my sorrows, oh! were great,
  Now all things look smiling;
Wonder not I feel elate,
  In your charms beguiling.

LX.

To Miss RILEY.

JUST a glimpse of a face as I passed,
    And the form quite a stranger to me,
Yet how deep an impression was cast
    On my heart that had ever been free.
I but met for a moment her eyes,
    And I felt how much havoc was done;
I passed on, but I knew by my sighs
    That my heart from my bosom was gone.

I may meet thee no more, dearest maid,
    Or, if so, it may be all in vain;
Yet in absence the flame will not fade,
    Though as strangers we ever remain.
Thine the form I shall think of the most,
    Thine the form I shall ever love best;
How I wish of thy love I could boast,
    And thy form by my own was possessed.

LXI.

To Miss McK.

HOW brightly shines the moon to-night,
   How soft the breezes blow,
While twinkling stars in heaven gleam bright,
   And bask in rills below.

My hand is clasped in hers I love—
   A maiden fair and young;
We hear the nightingale above
   Pour out its evening song.

In fervent vows I plight my troth,
   I hear her sweet reply :
" As loveth one so loveth both,
   Unchanging till we die.'"

LXII.

To — W——TON.

WHY weep, dear maid ? What sudden grief
   Thus makes your tear-drops flow ?
If I can give you sweet relief,
   Come, let me quickly know.
It grieves my heart to see a maid
   So fair as you in tears ;
Come, let me give you friendly aid,
   And ease you in your fears.

Yet what has made your pleasure fly,
   And sorrowed thus your heart ?
Have you had some fond parent die,
   Or brother from you part?
Or is there yet a dearer one
   From you now gone astray ?
If so, no other tear need run,
   Your grief can end to-day ;

For I will be your sweetheart, love,
   And prove both fair and true,
Nor will I ever from you rove,
   Or love maid aught but you.
Your present woe shall turn to bliss,
   Your sorrow take quick flight,
For we will sigh, and coo, and kiss,
   From morning until night.

LXIII.

To A. W.

IN spring, dear maid, the lark soars high,
    In summer, too, he loves to soar ;
His song resounds through autumn's sky,
    But winter hears his voice no more.

In spring the blackbird's song is sweet,
    But summer seldom hears him sing ;
Like nightingale's and cuckoo's greet,
    His song is heard but in sweet spring.

In spring the throstle sings his lays,
    In summer and in autumn, too ;
But in cold winter's cheerless days
    His song, like others, bids adieu.

A thousand gladsome birds beside,
    While days are bright, pour forth their praise ;
But few the winter drear can tide,
    Silent and hushed are then their lays.

Yet there is one whose song shall flow,
    However cold the winter be ;
As in spring, so in winter's snow,
    My song shall flow the same for thee.

LXIV.

To ——.

FAREWELL, my love; farewell, my dear;
  Adieu, my bonnie lass;
My bosom sighs, mine eye sheds tear,
  My heart near bursts, alas!
For well I know where'er I go
  No maid so dear can be;
I ne'er can meet a maid so sweet,
  So sweet a maid as thee.

My love shall burn like summer's sun
  In summer's brightest day,
Shall burn for one, and only one,
  While I am far away.
As points the compass to the pole
  My love shall turn to thee;
Thou shalt control both heart and soul
  Until I cease to be.

LXV.

To POLLY SMITH.

WHEN Sutton woods, so wild and free,
　　Do wear again their robes of green,
May I then wander there with thee,
　　And view the beauty of each scene ?

For though so fair those woods may be
　　To wander through when one's alone,
Yet doubly fair they'd seem with thee,
　　To whom this heart of mine hath flown.

With thee those woods would seem more free,
　　Each scene more beauteous would appear,
The songsters sing more sweet to me,
　　If thou wert there those songs to hear.

The boat upon the rippled lake
　　I would propel if thou didst need,
Or when we roved through glen and brake,
　　I'd see no thorn should make thee bleed.

So gentle maiden, let me hear
　　Thee say I shall roam there with thee,
And from that moment, oh, how dear
　　Will Sutton woods be held by me.

LXVI.

LOVE SONG.

THE morn was bright, the breezes light,
 And with sweet odour laden,
When in a lane, I, happy swain,
 Just happ'd to meet a maiden ;
Her eyes were blue, and her lip's hue
 Was redder than the cherry,
While from her tongue there came a song
 Which said her heart was merry.

I praised the strain, and wished again
 To hear the dainty ditty ;
Oh ! how she blushed, and would have rushed
 From me, without least pity,
But when I pressed her to my breast,
 And told my love's pure passion,
She paused awhile, then gave a smile,
 And took on me compassion.

Long years have passed, and time has cast
 Some furrows on my forehead,
Since she, and I, said fond good-bye,
 And breathed the tale love tempted.
Yet oft in sleep the tryst I keep,
 E'en as in days departed,
And in the lane I meet again
 The maid I left lone-hearted.

LXVII.

To SARAH S.

THOUGH joy is thine and grief be mine,
 As fate hath made it be,
Yet time shall come and blow strike home,
 And set me free, like thee.

'Tis for a time we breathe the clime
 Of sorrow and despair ;
'Tis for a time, though life-time's prime,
 This joy and bliss we share.

A few short years of smiles and tears
 And both of these must close,
And once for all in death's enthral
 As one we shall repose.

Till then I bear my sorrow's share,
 Nor murmur once again ;
But how reverse had been this curse
 Had I not loved in vain.

Then I with thee, and thou with me,
 We had kept side by side ;
Not, not as now, divided go,
 And tread life parted wide.

LXVIII.

A RETROSPECT.

I THINK of all the girls I've loved,
  And many, too, are they,
And find how few have faithful proved,
  How few love me to-day.

I think of all the girls I've loved,
  From first one to the last,
And find that nearly all have roved,
  And have love from them cast.

I think of all the maids I've loved,
  The false ones and the true,
And even now my heart is moved,
  To think on each adieu.

I think of all the maids I've loved,
  The dark ones and the fair,
And though by each I was beloved,
  How few of them I share.

I think of all the maids I've loved,
  The thin, stout, short, and tall,
And though to curse them, I've behoved
  A *blessing on them all.*

LXIX.

CHANGED OPINIONS.

I ONCE thought you a gentleman,
　　But now 'tis the reverse ;
I know you are as mean a man
　　As walks the universe.
I wonder if you ever went
　　In youth unto a school ;
If so, what time was then mis-spent
　　In sending such a ——.

To ——.

YOU bid me leave you—well, " good-bye,
　　Dear maid," I say to you ;
But know for sure that if I die,
　　'Twill be thro' this adieu,
For I could just as well exist
　　Without my breath as you.
" Oh well, come here, you shall be kissed,
　　And loved for loving true."

LOVE AND HATE.

LOVE with a woman is but a desire
　　That she can change as she feels joy or pain ;
But let her hate, her soul's one raging fire,
　　Which never lets her bosom love again.

LXX.

To F.

THE buttercup and daisy neat,
    Though simple gift may be,
Were to my heart a present sweet—
They proved you thought of me.
And though those flowers faded were,
    Their beauty all but o'er,
The blooming rose, or lily fair,
    Could not have been prized more.

LXXI.

To LOTTIE.

LET preachers make their sermons long,
    And point the way to heaven,
I know a quicker way, though wrong,
    That was unto me given.
This night I felt of Paradise,
    How looked the angels too.
It was, dear Lottie, when my eyes
    Looked on the form of you.

I cannot tell the thrill I felt
    When I was clasped by you ;
I dare not tell the bliss you dealt
    When I was loved so true.
Let preachers make their sermons long,
    And point the way to heaven,
The heaven I wish, however wrong,
    Is that which you have given.

LXXII.

To E.

THERE was a time, there was a time—
 I need not mention to thee now—
When Bradlow's Hill we used to climb
 And gaze with rapture from its brow.

There was a time I need not tell,
 It cannot be forgot by me
Till on this earth I cease to dwell,
 Till on this earth I cease to be.

There was a time I need not name
 Since 'twould not bring it back again,
When both our bosoms felt love's flame,
 Felt love in every pulse and vein.

There was a time, when side by side
 We used to sit in Bullon's Grove,
And in the cool of eventide
 List to the nightingale above.

There was a time, can I forget—
 However soon it may by thee—
When both our lips in kisses met,
 As though thy lips were made for me?

There was a time, when from thy tongue
 Came words which made my bosom glad,
Which made my heart with rapture strong,
 Nor knew my breast a feeling sad.

There was a time, but now 'tis gone,
 That time is changed, and so art thou ;
I wander now those scenes alone,
 For her I loved forgot each vow.

LXXIII.

CONSTANCY.

To HANNAH.

IT matters not how far or near
   Thy form and mine may ever be,
The same to me thou wilt be dear,
   The same I shall remember thee.

It matters not how distant I,
   This heart will still be true to thine ;
Love's flame in me can never die
   Till consciousness I do resign.

Though seas divide us, still my love,
   Dear maid, shall ever be thine own,
And tempters come, only to prove
   This heart is thine, and thine alone.

LXXIV.

To A——.

THY little nosegay, fair and sweet,
   I wear upon my breast,
That it may feel the constant beat
   Of that which loves thee best ;
And when it fades, as it must do,
   It shall be kept by me,
In memory of a maid loved true,
   In memory, dear, of thee.

LXXV.

To P.

I KNOW that our ears were given to us to hear,
  And our tongues that sweet speech we might speak,
Yet believe me, dear maid, what I speak is sincere,
  Though the language I use may be meek.

'Tis the duty of all to avoid telling lies,
  To avoid also hearing the same,
And for you to do both gives me pain and surprise,
  For I thought you were void of all blame.

You have spoken of one whom you never once saw,
  You have said ill of one never heard,
And to do so, believe me, indeed is a flaw,
  And in lady appeareth absurd.

It is easy, I know, to disparage a name,
  I have heard it is pleasant as well ;
If it be, I let others rejoice in such shame—
  Such a thing with me never shall dwell.

And believe me, dear maid, what I speak is the truth,
  And I hope it a warning will be,
For in life, though I never wronged maiden nor youth,
  Yet you see from abuse I'm not free.

So if this is the meed for one doing no wrong,
  How abused, then indeed, must I be,
So if ever the wish to give slander is strong,
  Why keep silent and think upon me.

LXXVI.

To CLARA.

WITHIN my breast there is a heart,
   And so there is in thine,
But oh, how different is its part
   Compared to this of mine,
How coldly it doth feel of love,
   And also unto me,
Whilst this of mine, like sun above,
   Doth burn and blaze for thee.

Is there no rapture in a kiss,
   Nor yet in clasp of hand ?
Doth thy white bosom feel no bliss,
   Nor to love's flame expand ?
If so, how diff'rent thou to me,
   Who deems such thing the best,
That Fate can give to mortals free
   To render us more blest.

LXXVII.

To E. W.

I NOW wish thee good bye, I now wish thee farewell,
   I now bid last adieu unto thee,
But remember, that long as on earth I may dwell
   Thou wilt ever be dearest to me.

For I love thee the fondest, I love thee the best,
   Though so short was the time I thee knew,
But one moment's enough for love's dart to pierce breast
   With a flame that is constant and true.

I may bid thee farewell, but farewell cannot make
   My lone heart think the less upon thee ;
Love, once felt by a bosom, will never forsake
   That same bosom till cold it shall be.

I may bid thee farewell, but farewell cannot change
   This fond heart which doth love thee alone ;
Though we meet not again, and though far I shall range,
   The same passion for thee I shall own.

I may bid thee adieu, but adieu will but fail
   To blot out all the pangs that are mine ;
If it could, oh, how soon would I let it avail,
   And forget that my heart is all thine.

But I cannot, and so to wish such would be vain ;
   I have loved, and must love still the same ;
And thy form is the one that inflicts the deep pain,
   'Tis for thee that I feel such a flame.

LXXVIII.

To E. W.

WHEN the moon shines in her glory
　　In the sky so clear,
Then the time to breathe love's story
　　To the one most dear.
When the moon rides high in splendour
　　Through the cloudless sky,
Then the time to breathe vow tender
　　And to heave love's sigh.

When the moon beams on the mountain,
　　And on lowly vale,
When she dances in the fountain,
　　Or lights quiet dale,
When she basks in sea and river,
　　Or in murm'ring rill,
Then the time to feel love's fervour,
　　Feel Cupid's sweetest thrill.

LXXIX.

To E. H.

ONLY one kiss I asked of thee,
  And yet I was denied ;
What little love was felt for me
  When rambling by thy side.

Thou tell'st me that when next we meet
  A kiss my lips shall gain,
Nor be denied the pleasant greet
  I asked to-day in vain.

Dear maid, we shall not meet again,
  Except by chance it be,
And even then I would not deign
  To ask a kiss from thee.

Yet do not deem no love I feel,
  Because these words are said,
Two shares I own of love's pure zeal—
  My own, *and thine*, dear maid.

If thou didst love me half as much
  As I, dear maid, do thee,
Thy lips on mine had left their touch,
  And happy had been me.

But farewell, maid ; thou canst not love
  My heart as I do thee ;
The flame I feel comes from above,
  It is so pure and free.

And though we may not meet again,
  Think not I shall forget
The maid I loved so well, though vain,
  The first time that we met.

LXXX.

To RUSSELL.

ACCEPT, dear friend, from me this cup,
    And often may'st thou toss it up
  Filled with the best prime ale—
Ale that will make the sad heart gay,
Ale that will drive all care away,
    And flush the cheek if pale.

And when thou drinkest the sweet draught
May the room re-echo with thy laugh
    To prove thy heart is light—
Light as the bird that carols forth
His daily song of joy and mirth
    Through all the summer bright.

And though I'm not well known to thee,
Still let the gift accepted be,
    Nor value it the less.
His friendship's true the cup who sends,
With him in death alone it ends,
    Wilt thou the same confess ?

LXXXI.

To Miss ——, Theatre.

IF all the wealth on earth were mine,
   And that in the blue sea,
One-half, dear maid, I would make thine
   To win thy heart from thee.

If all the wealth on earth were mine,
   And that in the deep sea,
The other half I would decline,
   If by such I gained thee.

But we are strangers, dearest maid,
   And still the same must be,
Yet mine the love that cannot fade,
   The love I feel for thee.

We meet, and part, as strangers do,
   No more each one to see ;
I leave behind my fond heart true,
   I leave it, maid, with thee.

LXXXII.

To S. F.

COME, tell me, lady, why thine eye
    Looks on me coldly now,
And why each time I pass thee by
    A frown comes o'er thy brow.
What have I done that I should lose
    The smiles I used to win ?
If I have err'd, do not refuse
    To tell me what's my sin.

Perhaps sland'ring tongues have spoken ill,
    And render'd black my name,
Or sworn it is my constant will
    To flirt with maid and dame.
Well, if they have, I must confess
    Their tongues spoke not a lie,
For sure 'tis my one happiness
    For every maid to sigh.

LXXXIII.

To Miss G.

A ROSE blooms sweet by Severn's side,
  And fair that rose is, too ;
Both far and near it is the pride—
  That rose, dear maid, is you.

I've roamed where thousand roses bloom,
  In many a varied hue,
Breathing their rich and sweet perfume,
  But none so sweet as you.

I hear that many prize your form,
  And love you fond and true,
Yet well I know no heart's so warm
  As this of mine for you.

Still must my passion blaze in vain,
  Tho' loving as I do,
For Fate decrees us to be twain,
  Tho' I love none but you.

So fare you well, my gentle maid,
  My fairest lass, adieu ;
Though far apart, love will not fade,
  Whilst I live I'll love you.

LXXXIV.

To POLLY SMITH.

I VIEW the lips mine own did kiss,
   A long, long time ago,
My heart remembers that same bliss,
   And wishes for it now.
I see the hand mine own once press'd,
   A long, long time ago,
I think of times when I was bless'd,
   And wish I was so now.

Oh, lady fair, time cannot change
   The love I felt of yore,
Though wedded thou, and tho' I range
   This wide world of ours o'er ;
It only bids me think of one
   Who is most dear to me,
It only bids me think of one,
   And that one only thee.

LXXXV.

PARTING.

To F. A.

MY heart felt true to bid adieu
   To friends and scenes so dear,
Till in the last embrace, so fast,
   I bade my sweetheart cheer.

Then seem'd my heart in two would part
   For giving her such woe,
Nor could I stay her sorrow's sway,
   Nor make less light the blow.

What sighs did rise, and in her eyes
   What teardrops rose and fell ;
In accents weak she tried to speak,
   Her tale of grief to tell.

It was in vain, too deep the pain ;
   She sank upon my breast,
And there as one our tears did run,
   Nor conquer I the test.

It was a sweet and cool retreat
   Where we bade that good-bye,
And on the night the moon rose bright,
   And show'd her tear-dimm'd eye.

The gentle breeze swept through the trees,
   And bore aloft her sigh,
The rill so fleet beneath our feet
   Seem'd sad as it \flow'd by.

At last, at last, farewell was past,
   The last fond kiss was given,
And, 'midst our tears, and latent fears,
   We parted with hearts riven.

And while this form with life is warm
   My love shall be sincere ;
Nor e'er forget love's faithful debt,
   But constant prove to her.

LXXXVI.

OLD FRIENDS.

WE may wander afar, and make friends not a few,
　　But they match not the dear ones of old;
They may love us as much, they may prove faithful, too,
　　Yet we cannot such love for them hold.
We may tender the hand, and may feel it be press'd
　　With a clasp that doth prove their love true ;
But for all this we feel the old friends are the best,
　　The old friends we in early days knew.

We may wander afar in some bright sunny clime,
　　And in pleasures forget all the past,
Yet a moment oft comes, and comes, too, at a time
　　When we seem in delight deepest cast,
And we think of the days, and the friendships gone by,
　　And we *feel* which were best and most true ;
It is answer'd too well by the deep render'd sigh,
　　That old friends are loved more than the new.

LXXXVII.

To Miss B.

WHY is the winter cold and chill ?
 Why is the summer warm and bright ?
Why is it spring the songsters thrill,
 And makes them carol, glad and bright ?

Why looks the spring so fresh and green ?
 Why do the flowers bloom so then ?
Why is it winter bares each scene,
 And makes so silent brake and glen ?

It is because in winter time
 Bright Phœbus rolls his course away,
It is because in summer's prime
 He comes again with bright long day.

The spring is green beneath his sway,
 The birds are glad within his sight,
And by his warm reviving ray
 The flowers bloom in sweet delight.

And what the sun is to the earth
 Thou art, dear lass, unto my heart,
For thou can'st give me summer's mirth,
 Or bid me feel cold winter's smart.

Miscellaneous.

I.

THE SONG OF THE WIND.*

OVER the mountains and hills far away,
    Over the valleys below ;
Over the main where the glad billows play,
With crests foaming white as blossoming May,
    Aye, matching the winter's snow.

I come and I go no mortal knows where,
    I'm free as freedom can be ;
I kiss the green meads where the buds bloom fair,
I carry their scent on the balmy air,
    I rustle the leaves with glee.

I linger awhile in the shady grove,
    I sigh through the leafy dell ;
I bear with me far the coo of the dove,
I carry the song from the lark above,
    And hymn from the nightingale.

I ripple the stream, I ruffle the rill,
    I plough o'er the ocean wide,
And the hearts of the strong with fear I fill,
Their bosoms with anguish and grief I thrill,
    As I sink their ships of pride.

Thus over the mountains and hills away,
    Such is the song that I sing ;
No spot on this earth but there do I stray,
I travel by night, I travel by day,
    I ride on a tireless wing.

---

* *Berrow's Worcester Journal*, August 25th, 1883.

II.

THE BROOK.*

I N some sweet nook near mountain high
    The rippling brook first meets the eye ;
Or in some dell where moonbeams play,
It breaks its spell and first sees day.

With birth so free its waters run
Right merrily 'neath glorious sun ;
Or stays to rest in flowery dale
To taste how blest the fragrant gale.

In turn through meads so fresh and green
Its pathway leads through many a scene ;
By shady wood where bluebell dwells
The little flood its murmur tells.

The violets blue and primrose pale
Like lovers true list to its tale ;
While songsters free 'neath shadows dim
There noiselessly the surface skim.

But onward still in dance and play
The rippling rill pursues its way ;
No scene, though fair, could be complete
If wanting there the brooklet sweet.

III.

CHRISTMAS.*

NOW doth stern winter hold his icy sway,
  And day flies quick, but lingers long the night ;
While through clear skies the pale moon takes her way,
  And stars and planets shine and twinkle bright.

'Tis Christmas Eve ! and on the stilly air
  Rich music floats in harmony most sweet,
While every bosom some joy seems to share,
  And young and old around the bright hearth meet.

The song resounds, goes round the brimming glass,
  The burning log gives out a ruddy glow ;
Now gallant youth breathes love to fairest lass,
  While blushes she to hear the fervent vow.

A merry time is this old Christmas Day,
  When pleasure reigns, and woe is made depart :
The poor and humble, like the rich, feel gay,
  And bliss sincerest dwells within each heart.

Now ye who have wealth at your own command,
  Come, let it flow, and help grim poverty ;
The good 'twill give when it hath left your hand
  Will bring ye pleasure, and ease misery ;
Aye, doubly glad will Christmas Day go by
With those who save a fellow-creature sigh.

* *Berrow's Worcester Journal,* December 25th, 1880.

IV.

BILLY.*

A LITTLE mound in churchyard green :
    A few sweet flowers fair
Upon that grassy mound are seen,
    Scenting the neighb'ring air.
'Tis passed by all with careless eye,
    No grief pervades their breasts ;
But far away two bosoms sigh,
    For here their baby rests.

Two laughing eyes of azure blue,
    Two lips like cherries red,
Bright shining locks of auburn hue
    Twined round his little head ;
Two dimpled hands (now gently crossed
    Upon his snowy breast)—
Such was the little lad we lost,
    Who 'neath that mound doth rest.

Shall we forget the knowing gaze
    He seemed to give us both,
(When faded fast life's feeble blaze,)
    And told the coming truth?
It said too well we should not keep
    The flower we loved so well ;
Yet know we as our tears we weep
    Such buds in heaven do dwell.

* *Worcester Herald*, July 14th, 1883.

V.

THE HUNTER.

A YOUNG hunter rode forth on a bright winter's morn,
  To give chase to the fleet-footed deer,
And he cracked loud his whip, and he blew loud his horn,
  With a note that was merry and clear ;
And he sang a glad lay as he went on his way,
  And he whistled a gay, thrilling tune,
For his spurs they were bright, and his heart it was light,
  Aye, as light as a skylark's in June.

" Come away, come away," was the song that he sung,
  " Come away to the woodland and lea.
Let your courser be fleet, let your courser be strong,
  Or you will not the death of stag see ;
He is nimble of foot, and his wind it is clear,
  And he'll lead us a long bonny ride,
But with horse and with hound of the best never fear,
  We shall see how the noble stag died."

VI.

To THERESA (Byron's "Maid of Athens").*

As flowers bloom, and then decay,
So do we mortals pass away.

LIKE him who praised her in the past so well
   In verse and language ne'er on earth to die,
Has she now bid this life its long farewell,
   And in the cold and gloomy tomb must lie ;
   But where the charms that made the poet sigh,
The swelling breast in colour like the snow,
   The rosy cheek, the bright and sparkling eye,
(To match it which Gazelle alone could show,)
And all the charms that made his verse to flow ?

Faded long since ; and could he see her now,
   I warrant me he'd doubt she was the same
Who bade his bosom in the past to glow,
   And in a host of others put love's flame ;
   But not with her through such doth rest the blame,
For time will mar the glories of the best,
   And take them soonest—though it seems a shame
That Beauty cannot with us ever rest,
And make us sons of toil be longer bless'd.

But fare thee well, Theresa, once so gay,
   No one so lovely in their youth as thou :
Through all the land thy beauty held its sway,
   Long after him who sang it was laid low,
   While, with thy charms Worth, too, adorned thy brow,
And prov'd the owner good as she was fair.
   Thy name will perish not while Britons know
Childe Harold's song, and that will last for e'er ;
What woman's fate with thine then will compare ?

---

* Died March, 1881.

VII.

HUMILITY.

HOW lowly builds the lark his nest,
  And yet how high he soars ;
How plainly is the throstle dressed,
  And yet what song he pours.
The little linnet in the glade,
  And nightingale so shy,
How humbly are these songsters clad,
  Yet sweet their melody.

The modest violet in the dell,
  With petals scarcely shown,
The cowslips which in meadows dwell,
  What fragrance these do own,
The honeysuckle, wild and free,
  How sweet its odour, too,
The rose may queen of flowers be,
  She's richest but in hue.

Thus worth may wed simplicity,
  Not deck itself with pride ;
A pattern we can always see
  In nature's field so wide.
'Tis joy to meet a noble mind,
  Find soft heart in rough breast,
When worth and meekness are combined,
  Each shows itself at best.

VIII

FRIENDSHIP.

LET morning dawn, let twilight fade,
  Let dark night pass, morn dawn again,
Let day and night thus change, dear maid,
  But ne'er let friendship be in twain.

Let gentle spring, with mantle green,
  Make earth look fair beneath her reign,
While birds with glad songs hail her queen,
  But ne'er let friendship be in twain.

Let summer come and give the bloom
  To every flower on the plain,
While every breeze breathes sweet perfume,
  But ne'er let friendship be in twain.

Let autumn follow with full hand,
  And load the earth with fruit and grain,
Which rustics reap in many a band,
  But ne'er let friendship be in twain.

Let winter come with blast and cold,
  Let winter come with grief and pain,
But do not let him gain thy fold,
  To make our friendship be in twain.

Let years fly by, with sloth, or speed,
  And try to part the tie in vain,
Till both our hearts by death are freed,
  Then may our friendship be in twain.

IX.

WILD FLOWERS.*

THEIR breath comes floating on each gale
    From distant valleys green ;
Their presence gladdens hill and dale,
    And beautifies each scene.
The cowslip, with its crown of gold,
    The primrose pale in hue,
The daisy neat, and bluebell bold,
    Each helps to make the view.

On hedgerow green the May-bloom shows ;
    In copse hide violets sweet ;
The yellow gorse on moorland glows,
    And buttercups give greet.
From meadow low to mountain high
    Bright buds are blossoming,
They waft sweet odours to the sky,
    And tell us " This is spring !"

* *Worcester Herald*, June 30th, 1883.

X.

THE ROVER.

I AM a rover, young and gay,
  And glad as glad can be,
For be it night, or be it day,
  I roam with footsteps free.
The rocky hill, the mountain high,
  The pleasant valley low,
The shady dale where flowers lie,
  Are sweetest things I know.

I love the rill where moon-rays beam,
  Or basks the sun from high ;
I sit beside the flowing stream
  And hear the willows sigh ;
I view the leaves on hedgerow green,
  With flowers in the meads ;
I note how lovely is each scene
  Where Nature beauty spreads.

I love to hear the songsters sing,
  And think how glad they are ;
I love to hear the lark loud ring
  His carol in the air ;
I love to hear the piping thrush
  And blackbird's note so clear ;
The linnet warbling in the bush,
  And philomela dear.

Some value wealth, some value fame,
  I envy them no jot ;
Within my breast burns brighter flame,
  And sweeter makes life's lot.
To roam the earth so changing fair,
  To ride the boundless sea,
Is every joy I wish to share,
  For I'm a rover free

XI.

HIS WIFE.

I SAT me down one summer's day
  Upon a hillock green ;
A maiden chanced to come that way,
  The fairest ever seen.
I raised my hat, and said, "Good morn !"
  She blushed, and said the same ;
I told her that I felt forlorn,
  And burned with love's pure flame.

She blushed deep red, and heaved a sigh,
  And said she felt so, too ;
I whispered I could for her die,
  Could she but love me true.
I kissed her lip so crimson hued,
  And clasped her to my breast ;
That meeting I have never rued,
  For wife she made the best.

We often talk of that one day,
  Although so long ago,
When we first met, both young and gay,
  And felt our bosoms glow.
We feel that if by some decree
  We were once more made twain,
What we are now we still would be,
  Would meet and wed again.

XII.

MEMORY.

THOUGH youth may fly on pinions fleet,
    And joys may pass away,
There still remains dear memory sweet
    To cheer us on our way.

The friends we knew and loved so true
    May part, nor meet again ;
Yet memory lasts our lifetime through,
    And makes less deep the pain.

The thrill we felt in youth may die,
    With other joys depart ;
Yet memory stays to ease the sigh,
    And cheer the lonely heart.

With memory's aid we press hand warm
    That has long lain in death.
We once more clasp the well-loved form,
    And hear the long-lost breath.

We still can kiss the ruby lip
    And bask in beaming eyes ;
Time only can our pleasures nip
    When memory in us dies.

XIII.

HOPE.

WHAT would this life be, dearest maid,
      Without sweet hope to lead us on ?
How often would the heart be sad,
      And faithful bosoms feel most lone.
If hope, dear maid, calmed not the breast,
      How dreary would life's pathway be ;
'Tis balm by which grief is supprest,
      And renders hearts more glad and free.

'Tis hope, dear maid, that gives me joy,
      And bids me seek to win thy heart ;
'Tis hope, dear maid, that stays the sigh
      That oft would from my bosom start ;
'Tis hope, dear maid, that gives me cheer,
      That stranger I not long may be ;
'Tis hope, dear maid, that drowns my fear,
      And bids me think thou'lt feel for me.

XIV

WOMAN'S CHARMS.

TO paint the ray from woman's eye
Must be a pleasing task ;
But sweeter far, none can deny,
In that same ray to bask.

To paint the red of woman's lip
Must be sweet work indeed ;
But sweeter far the dew to sip
From off that lip so red.

It must be sweet to paint the white
Of woman's spotless breast ;
But how much greater the delight
To be unto it pressed !

XV.

THE MOUNTAINEER.

SOME love to dwell in smoky town,
  Some love the fair country ;
Some love the valley, some the down,
  Some love to ride the sea ;
But give to me the mountain high,
  Where blow the breezes free ;
No heart of mountaineer can sigh,
  Then mountain high for me !

On mountain's brow the dawn first breaks,
  There rising sun first shines ;
And when at eve he earth forsakes
  His last ray there reclines.
There falls the rain, there falls the snow,
  There shines the sunshine free ;
There breezes fresh for ever blow,
  Then mountain high for me !

XVI.

THE MOONLIGHT HOUR.

SOME love the hour when sun first beams
　　On mountain, hill, and tree ;
But though to some this sweetest seems,
　　It does not so to me.

Some love the hour when high above
　　The sun shines glad and free ;
I know an hour I better love—
　　There's hour more dear to me.

Some love the hour when in the west
　　The sun sinks o'er the sea,
And in one blaze the heavens are dressed ;
　　Yet such is not by me.

Some love the hour when twilight calm
　　Fills heaven's canopy ;
To some such hour is sweetest balm ;
　　It is not such to me.

Give me the hour when in the sky
　　The moon shines merrily ;
That is the hour with maid to sigh,
　　That is the hour for me.

XVII.

THE ROVER.

WHERE sucks the wild bee there roam I,
　　Through many a flow'ry dell;
Green mead, from whence soars lark to sky,
　　There do I roam as well.
I love to bask 'neath summer's sun
　　And breathe the breezes sweet;
I love to watch the brooklets run
　　In ripples at my feet.

Where sucks the wild bee there roam I,
　　Through meadow, copse, and lea;
O'er lowly plain, up mountain high,
　　'Tis all the same to me.
I love to sit in shady grove
　　And tell love's fervent tale;
And, while the moonbeams dance above,
　　List to the nightingale.

XVIII.

DAWN.

TWILIGHT's fair, but dawn is fairer
    When it breaks in cloudless sky;
Birds' songs clear in dawn trill clearer
    Than when gloomy night is nigh.

Twilight's still, but dawn is stiller,
    Hushed is all but Nature's sound;
E'en the mill, where lives the miller,
    Hath not yet commenced its round.

Twilight's soft, but dawn is softer,
    Who can speak or paint its view?
Dawn's the hour to rove wild bower,
    And hear lark o'er fields of dew.

Twilight's sweet, but dawn is sweeter;
    Summer's bright, spring's brighter still;
Joy is fleet, but youth is fleeter,
    E'en as torrent is to rill.

XIX.

A ROMANCE.

SWEET Nellie was the fairest maid
  In all the village green ;
And stranger Will the noblest lad
  Round all the country seen.
Their hearts were light as hearts could be,
  Both lov'd each other true ;
A fairer couple none could see,
  E'en though they roam'd earth through.

And when the happy morning came
  Which gave him her as bride,
And pledges proved how true the flame
  Which did in each reside,
The village lads, and lasses too,
  Turn'd out in glad array,
In song and dance all merry grew
  Till spent the summer day.

" Thy home, dear wife, is not yon cot,
  Though sweet, perchance, it be ;
A better and a nobler lot
  Has been well won by thee.
I am not poor, nor lowly born,
  As thou and all did ween ;
Thy country's crown doth me adorn,
  And thou art now its queen."

XX.

TO A CAGED SKYLARK.

UNHAPPY bird ! I pity thee,
   For though so sweet thy song may flow,
While thus confined, how well I know
Thy heart must pine for liberty.

'Tis true thou viewest the blue sky,
   But that must make thee grieve the more
   To think thou canst not in it soar,
And pour thy thrilling song on high.

Thy place is in the meadow green,
   Where flowers wild make sweet the air,
   Where glen and rill make earth look fair,
And freedom sweet dwells on each scene.

Sing on, sad lark, nor yet in vain,
   For by the song that thou dost sing
   We know that once more come is spring,
And verdure decks the earth again.

XXI.

NELLIE AND NED.—A Love Tale.

THE morn was bright, June's sunny beam
    Made lovely bright the weather,
When on the banks of gentle Teme
    Two lovers strolled together ;
The one was Ned, a gallant lad,
    The other fairest Nellie—
Two fonder hearts earth never had,
    And never will, I tell ye.

They watched the crystal water run
    Through meadows green and smiling,
They watched the lark soar in the sun,
    And heard his song beguiling ;
They watched the light-winged swallow skim
    Through skies of purest azure,
No cloud was seen the sun to dim,
    Or make less glad their pleasure.

With smile Ned said, "The day is hot,
    In th' river I will bathe me,
So rest awhile, nor leave this spot,
    I'll soon return, dear, to thee."
Some distance up the river side
    He there did quick undress him ;
Where willow bushes did him hide,
    The river did caress him.

Nell heard the plunge her lover gave
    With short and merry laughter,
She looked to see him stem the wave
    And rise from the deep water.
She looked in vain, for never more
    Returned to her her lover,
For they who dragged the river o'er
    Did his cold form discover.

In churchyard green poor Ned lies now,
    And Nellie sleeps beside him,
She could not bear the bitter blow,
    And battle life denied him.
A humble stone now marks the spot
    Where they sleep near each other ;
How many a youth sighs at their lot,
    And weeps his gentle lover.

XXII.

THE SKYLARK.

SOAR, skylark, soar, for winter drear is past,
The joyful spring has come again at last,
Tho' none need tell thee, for thou wast the first
Who winter's silence and long suffering burst.

Soar, skylark, soar, rise high on buoyant wing
And give a welcome with thy note to spring,
While others listen to thy thrilling voice
And wish (tho' vain) they could like thee rejoice.

Soar, skylark, soar, 'tis long since thou wast heard
'Mongst fleecy clouds where sings no other bird,
For with cold winter and its months so long
Thou didst forget the tune of thy glad song.

Soar, skylark, soar, the grass again is green,
The leaves with beauty clothe each woodland scene,
The frozen rill has broken winter's sway,
And o'er the plain now tinkles on its way.

The flowers wild in many a varied hue
Bloom in the sun and sparkle with night's dew,
While hill and dale, that lately looked so bare,
Have robed themselves in mantle fresh and fair.

So, skylark, soar, and still while soaring sing,
And make the welkin with thy music ring,
For well we know while hearing thy notes true,
That spring has come, and winter says Adieu.

XXIII.

A REPROOF.

To Miss N.

'TIS not the bird that sweetest sings
    That boasts best plumage too ;
For heed the lark which gladly rings
    His song in sky of blue ;
Or, sweeter yet, the nightingale,
    Which sings when fled the day ;
The humble linnet in the dale,
    How plainly dressed are they !

The buds that have the sweetest smell
    Boast not the fairest hue.
In spring so green search but the dell
    Where blooms the violet blue.
Compare its fragrance to the rose,
    Which is with beauty blest ;
How sweet is that the violet knows,
    Although so humbly dressed.

The roughest ore contains the gold,
    The sparkling gem as well ;
And many a heart that's true and bold
    In poor clad breast may dwell.
Beauty is sweet, but *worth* is more,
    And ever will be, too ;
When beauty conquers merit o'er,
    Time then to bid adieu.

XXIV.

YOUTH.

THE star that shines the first at eve
Is oft the last at morn to leave,
The ray it gives perchance most bright
Of all the host that shine at night ;
And oft in life it happens, too,
The first thrill felt bids last adieu ;
The first thrill, too, p'rhaps best of all
We ever felt, or ever shall.
In youth we think of love and wealth ;
In youth we feel of strength and health ;
We feel our bosom glow and swell
Beneath the power of beauty's spell ;
We love to bask in sunny rays
Which do from woman's bright eyes blaze ;
We love to kiss the ruby lip,
And all the dew from off it sip ;
We love to hear the tender vow
Which tongue of maiden will let flow ;
We love to view the spotless breast,
And feel the thrill when to it prest ;
We idle on, and think, and deem
That ne'er can fade the blissful dream ;
Think that, as future years go by,
Such joy and bliss will never die.
Deceitful thought ! when youth has fled,
How soon the other joys are dead ;
How vain each wish for strength and health,
How impotent the greatest wealth.
Wealth may win ray from woman's eye,
Wealth, too, may woman's kisses buy,
May even win the breast like snow,
But ne'er the thrill that youth doth know,—
When that is fled, 'tis ever gone ;
The others make us but more lone,
And bid us feel the loss the more
Of joys we owned in days of yore.
So love sweet youth as best you may,
It comes no more once pass'd away ;
And know for sure, its joys are best
Of all that are in life possess'd.

XXV.

TIME.

HOW swiftly time takes wing :
    It seems but yesterday
We plucked the buds of spring,
    Now winter holds his sway.

How swiftly time takes flight :
    It seems an hour ago
We basked in summer bright,
    Now wintry breezes blow.

How swiftly flies old time :
    It seems but as this morn
We roamed in autumn prime,
    Now winter reigns forlorn.

And thus, with life the same ;
    It passes like a dream ;
A sudden ray, a fickle flame,
    Then quenched in Lethe's stream.

XXVI.

SERENADE.

AWAKE! awake! my lady fair,
Thy lover true is near;
Awake! while on the midnight air
Comes music soft and clear.
I'll tune my harp, and sing my song,
In praise of one so dear;
Awake! I will not tarry long;
Awake! and music hear.

The stars are twinkling in the sky,
Awake! and see them shine;
The moon is sailing bright on high,
Awake! fair lady mine.
I'll tune my harp, and sing my lay,
In praise of only thee;
Farewell! for yonder dawns the day;
Sleep, love, and dream of me.

XXVII.

LOVE.

THERE is pleasure in spring, and in summer-time, too,
    There is pleasure in autumn so full ;
There is pleasure in winter, though cold is its view,
    Which will save the fond heart feeling dull ;
There is joy in each season, whatever it be,
    Which will ever the hours beguile,
For what matters the season to any, or me,
    If we bask in a maiden's bright smile ?

Meadows green may be fair, summer's scenes may be sweet,
    Autumn's fruits may be luscious to taste ;
And there may be a joy when the snow and the sleet
    Cast a mantle o'er mountain and waste ;
But such joys will not equal the joy of a smile,
    Or a kiss from a maiden's lips red,
For although such sweet bliss may oft lead on to guile,
    In such pleasure all sorrow is fled.

XXVIII.

MORNING.

THE stars have faded in the sky,
　　The moon has sunk to rest,
And healthful breezes freshly sigh
　　O'er hill and mountain crest.
The lark shakes from his wings the dew
　　That gathered there at night,
And, singing, soars in realms of blue
　　To hail the morning bright.

The blackbird leaves his cosy nest
　　To give his morning lay ;
The bee wakes from his drowsy rest
　　And seeks the flow'ry way.
The very rill seems to rejoice
　　While murm'ring o'er the plain,
And meads to lend a thankful voice,
　　That morn has come again.

XXIX.

CHRISTMAS NIGHT.

COME, sit around the fire bright,
   And join the jovial throng,
We'll let the dreary winter's night
   Go by in dance and song.
We'll fill the glass and let it pass
   Till merry grows each heart,
While gallant youth and blushing lass
   Their love vows do impart.

Pile on the log and let it burn
   Till ruddy is its glow ;
Let music banish sorrow stern,
   And let the glad song flow.
Let hearts unite this Christmas night,
   And give each other joy ;
No night like this for weal and bliss,
   No time to-night to sigh.

XXX.

THE PORTRAIT.

HERE 's my carté, dearest maid, and right welcome you are
  To the gift which I give unto you ;
But I grieve that the *image* alone is your share—
  Not my heart, and my bosom so true.
Yet these two had been yours, like the portrait is now,
  If you for their possession had sought,
For how much for your bosom mine own did once glow,
  And how deeply you dwelt in each thought.

XXXI.

SAILOR'S SONG.

THE morn is bright, the breeze is light,
　　My ship is staunch and true,
So come with me, and roam the sea,
　　I have a merry crew.
I'll set my sail before the gale,
　　We'll have a bonny ride ;
　　I only need a sailor's meed,
　　A fair maid for my bride.

Oh ! say not nay; let's speed away,
　　My ship is waiting near,
She'll stem the tide, with gallant pride,
　　Her crew owns not a fear ;
With thee as bride to grace my side,
　　I shall not own a care ;
This wide, fair earth shall find us mirth,
　　If thou the voyage wilt share.

XXXII.

To BOB.

SO, Bob, thou'rt caught at last
    In Hymen's tangled net ;
Thy freedom's reign is past,
    Perchance not with regret ;
For many a broil was thine
    In days of single bliss,
At least, if 'twas like mine ;
    Now, do I guess amiss ?

But since the web thou'st wove,
    And round thee cast the chain,
I hope the change will prove
    All pleasure, without pain.
I often wish I were,
    Bob, in the state like thee,
For then I should oft share
    Rest rarely felt by me.

But risk I scarcely dare
    The yoke of married state,
However rich and fair
    May be the would-be mate.
I choose to rest awhile,
    And, single, still be free ;
Thy turn may come to smile
    To see me cag'd like thee.

XXXIII.

ON LOSING A FRIEND.

G. T.

OF thee, harsh Fate, I would complain
　　At this thy cruel, unkind blow,
Did I not know 'twould be in vain,
And that 'twas heav'n who willed it so.
If not for this thou shouldst be curst
With curse the deepest, and the worst,
And on thy ever dreaded name
I would cast deep and bitter shame.
But though the blow which thou hast dealt
Seems cruel and unkind to all,
Though it hath made our fond hearts melt,
And hot tears from our eyelids fall,
'Tis still our duty to forbear,
And bind our grief to sigh and tear.
Yet oh ! how sad to bid farewell
To those we love, and love so well ;
How sad to bid the last adieu
To those we love, and love so true.
Well may our bosoms heave the sigh,
And tears bedim the friendly eye ;
To see one meet such early death,
And gone for ever life's sweet breath,
Ere half the years o'er him had flown
Which God decreed man's race should own.
But it hath proved the proverb true,
"The best are first to bid adieu ; "
For who had nobler mind than he,
Whose heart more generous, or more free ?
Whose tongue so gentle in its speech,
Whose thoughts grasp more within their reach ?
Whose pencil trace sweeter outline ;
Whose brush make sun more brightly shine ?
The grassy field, the hedgerow green ;
The sparkling brook, the mountain scene,

The grazing cattle, bird on wing ;
The lovely flowers in the spring ;
The azure clear of summer sky,
The wintry blasts and storms on high,
His hand made real unto the eye :
That hand is cold, its work is done,
The will that guided it is flown,
And ere the sought-for fame was won,
Which had he lived he sure had known,—
The struggle his, but not the praise
Which Fate at some less worthy lays.
He climbed the hill, but fell before
The top was reached, with all its store ;
He stemmed the tide, but sunk before
His feet could touch the courted shore ;
And all the meed his genius won
Was toil and labour, pleasure none :
An early grave the one reward
For days and nights of struggles hard.
The churchyard cold is now his home.
But, if there is a heav'n above,
His spirit in that heav'n will roam
In endless peace and endless love.
And though with us he now is not,
He cannot be by us forgot :
Too dear the friend in him we knew,
For memory e'er to bid adieu.
No future joy, nor old time yet,
Makes less our sorrow or regret ;
But rather, as the years fly o'er,
Makes us more grieve, and more deplore
That he could not with us remain
And give the fruits of heart and brain.
But 'twas God's will that he should die,
And so He call'd his soul on high—
A soul too good on earth to rest ;
By souls like his is heav'n made blest,
But only those who know such here
Can guess how much such friends are dear.

XXXIV.

L OVE but beams in maiden's eyes
   The heart of youth to flatter ;
And when his bosom deeply sighs,
   Then all his fond hopes scatter.

But should he fail to sigh at all,
   And scorn such foolish cooing,
How soon she will at his feet fall
   And do both shares of wooing.

XXXV.

WOMAN AND WINE.

L IFE is short, therefore, let it be merry,
    Let it pass like the summer time bright,
Kissing lips which outvie the ripe cherry,
    Pressing bosoms so soft and so white.
Life is short, therefore, let us shun sorrow,
    Let us happiness win while we may,
For who knows but it may be to-morrow
    That shall prove to us all the last day ?

There is pleasure for all who will seek it,
    There is sorrow for those who will bear ;
But here's one, and mine own tongue shall speak it,
    Of the latter will not have a share.
There are lovely, fond maids to caress us,
    There is wine, too, to cheer us when sad,
Even these prove how much God doth bless us,
    And how much He would have us be glad.

So here's health to the fond, loving lasses !
    And all hail to the red cheering wine !
For their joy every other surpasses,
    So at least thinks this glad heart of mine.
I have tried every pleasure enticing,
    And have proved these two ever the best,
Aye, no other was ever worth prizing,
    It is woman and wine make us blest.

XXXVI.

RURAL SCENES.

TO saunter by the rippling rill,
　　To ramble o'er the flow'ry mead,
To climb the mountain high, or hill,
　　To me is pleasant work indeed.

'Tis sweet to sit in shady grove
　　When leaves are green in smiling spring
And listen to the gentle dove,
　　And to the birds that gaily sing.

'Tis sweet to wander by the stream
　　When summer's sun is shining bright,
And watch the ripples dance and gleam
　　Like countless stars on winter's night.

'Tis sweet to ride the boundless sea
　　Or ramble on its sandy shore,
And watch the billows wild and free,
　　And listen to their mighty roar.

This earth is fair to those who choose
　　To view it with contented eye,
But how much joy those mortals lose
　　Who think not beauteous earth and sky.

XXXVII.

FIRST LOVE.

OH, he came and went a stranger,
　　But he left on my heart trace,
For I knew not then the danger
　　For poor maid to view such face ;
But that face was fair and smiling,
　　And his voice was rich and sweet,
Oh, those moments how beguiling,
　　And in passing, oh, how fleet.

It is long years since I met him,
　　And we may not meet again,
But my heart will not forget him,
　　Though my love may be in vain.
I have met, and may meet many
　　Who'll be fair as fair can be,
But I never shall meet any
　　Half so dear as he to me.

XXXVIII.

DREAMS OF YOUTH.

To BOB.

DEAR Bob, we roam again no more
 The pleasant scenes of youth so gay ;
Nor ramble, as we did of yore,
 To Bullon's Grove at dawn of day.

Each scene so fair, though not forgot,
 These eyes of mine no longer view ;
Chang'd now, alas ! Bob, is my lot,
 To them, and thee I've bid adieu.

No more, dear Bob, my footsteps tread
 Up Doghill steep, or Bradlow high,
And ere the sun a beam hath shed
 Watch dawning break in eastern sky.

And others, too, we both once knew,
 Who with us then with light hearts rov'd,
Have, like me, bid a last adieu
 To scenes which must be ever lov'd.

The scenes I view may be as fair
 As those I've left so far away,
But not such joy for them I share,
 Their beauty fails to make me gay.

Yet, though deep seas now us divide,
    In dreams those seas are often pass'd,
And often, Bob, still side by side
    We roam again as in the past.

Yes, oft in sleep I traverse o'er
    Each verdant hill and leafy glade,
And feel the joyous heart of yore
    When deem'd I youth would never fade.

Oft, oft in sleep I dream I rove,
    Bob, by thy side, as oft I've done ;
Nor feels my breast a pang to prove
    That those days are for ever gone.

And if a time should come again
    When those scenes once more I may view,
To me it will but be with pain,
    For gone the friends my childhood knew.

The sun may shine, and look as bright,
    And still as fair may seem each scene,
But could this heart of mine beat light
    To view *alone* where we have been ?

XXXIX.

THE BOWL.

THAT man's a fool whoe'er supposes
   Life is but a bed of roses,
Since every joy fair women give
Is but a salve to bid us live.
For what with endless trials and crosses,
The ups and downs, the gains and losses,
What tongue can say life has no thorn
To make us feel for it some scorn ?

Yet there's one joy above all others,
Which surely every sorrow smothers,
And 'tis to quaff the brimming bowl,
When woe will fly the heart and soul.
It matters not what pains may grieve us,
The sparkling bowl will soon relieve us ;
Come weal, come woe, whiche'er it be,
The glorious wine bowl pass to me.

XL.

THE REFUSAL.

To B. W. L.

TIME may be fleeting, and thy hand
   May have too much to do,
Yet did thy heart the wish command,
How soon, as from a wizard's wand,
   Had Berwick rose in view.

Yea, as no other hand could trace
   Or paint that scene so fair,
For 'tis where Severn runs her race
With sister Teme, near Berwick's place,
   We both breathe native air.

But I am poor, and humble too,
   And thou art rich and great,
No need then for thy hand to do
The little favour sought from you—
   Well, I abide my fate.

XLI.

L O V E .

L OVE is a joy that never dies,
　　But lasteth through all time ;
Nor does it fade, as life's spark flies,
　　Nor chills in coldest clime ;
But glows the same on Greenland's strand
As on far Afric's arid sand.

And when man's heart hath ceas'd to beat,
　　When cold the body lies,
At once it makes a passage fleet
　　Through boundless azure skies—
To wait until the trump's loud strain
Shall bid us each one love again.

XLII.

To ——.

WHAT gift is half so priz'd as *love?*
    What else on earth to man so dear?
What feeling will so quickly move
    His heart with throb of joy or fear?

When absent from the one we choose
    How soon beats low the loving heart;
The bosom will each joy refuse,
    While sigh and tear alone will start.

But when two faithful lovers meet,
    What feelings in their bosoms dwell;
Then does each heart in that fond greet
    Beat as 'twould burst its very cell.

XLIII.

THE miser dreams his dream of gold,
  The spendthrift dreams his dream of waste,
The warrior dreams of battle bold,
  Or yearns that morning would but haste ;
The poet dreams of lasting name,
  The sculptor of his noble art,
The painter of a mighty fame,
  Which once earned never may depart.

I envy not the dream of wealth,
  The miser's dream of hoarded gain ;
Nor yet the spendthrift's loss of health,
  Whichever follows in his train ;
But with the others I can vie,
  My dreams surpass their own I prove,
If not, why then my dream must lie,
  But can it, when it is of *love ?*

The miser's gold is soonest spent,
  The spendthrift's life doth soonest end,
The soldier's blood is but mis-spent
  In making fellow-mortals bend ;
The poet's name may ages last,
  The marble may by storm be riven,
The painter's canvas may fade fast,
  But *love* is not of earth, but heaven.

XLIV.

A LOVE TALE.

THE squire was rich, and his daughter fair,
  And gay suitors she had many a one ;
They were rich and great, but she did not care,
  In secret her heart was already won.

The squire was vexed that she would not wed
  With the lord he'd chosen to be her mate ;
What cared he for the tears his daughter shed ?
  The suitor was rich, and his title great.

The sun rose brightly on the bridal day,
  But for him, and his hopes, it rose in vain ;
The maiden had fled in the dawning gray
  To him who lived over the distant main.

Not her father's wealth, nor position high,
  Could displace from her heart the love it knew,
And poor though his purse she should heave no sigh,
  But be happy with him she loved best and true.

XLV.

WHERE the eagle wheels his flight,
      And the snow lies pure and white,
Nor melts 'neath summer's ray ;
Or where brooklets murm'ring flow
In the valley green below,
      'Tis there I love to stray.

Where the breeze blows fresh and free
O'er the blue and rolling sea,
      'Tis there I love to ride ;
Or to bask upon the shore
And list to the wild waves' roar
      At each succeeding tide.

In the cool and leafy dale,
In the open verdant vale,
      'Tis there I love to rove,
While the thrush pipes loud his song,
And the lark pours carol strong,
      Or nightingale its love.

But the time I love to stray
Is when laughing moonbeams play
      On river, lake, and sea ;
For 'tis then my bosom glows,
When I hear the fervent vows
      Told by one dear to me.

Oh ! this life is short and sweet,
And they say that heaven is sweet,
      Since mortals wish them there ;
But this earth is heaven to me,
And the same will ever be,
      While I these joys can share.

XLVI.

LOVE.

BRIGHT are the rays that Phœbus throws
 Through summer's azure skies,
But not so bright by far as those
 Which come from maiden's eyes.

Red is the hue that cherries own,
 And coral in the sea,
But redder still I've often known
 On maid's lip dear to me.

Rich is the bloom fair roses show
 When they are at their best,
But I have seen a richer glow
 By maiden's cheek possessed.

White is the snow on plain or height
 When winter reigns supreme,
But maiden's breast I've seen as white,
 Aye, whiter oft would seem.

So who will wonder why I prize
 Fair lassie as I do?
Unhappy he who can despise
 A gem with charms so true.

XLVII.

LOVE SONG.

WHO can frown when woman smiles ?
   No one in his senses ;
Who would notice half their wiles
   When love recompenses ?
One soft ray from woman's eye
   Well repays the seeking ;
One sweet kiss will kill each sigh,
   Though a heart were breaking.

Who can frown when woman smiles ?
   No one without grieving ;
Who will not forget their wiles,
   Though they are deceiving ?
Every pang a woman gives
   She can heal at pleasure ;
In their keeping rest our lives,
   And *love* life's dearest treasure.

XLVIII.

LOVE.

LOVE may burn, and love may fade
   In many a fond believer,
But there was never youth or maid
   But proved love a deceiver.

Love may fade, and love may burn
   In maiden, wife, or widow,
But, as in man, they all must learn
   Love is at best a shadow.

Sweet is love, when he is true,
   And bliss 'tis to caress him ;
But on this earth, oh ! what a few
   Can all through life possess him.

Love will fade, and love will glow
   In turn to-day—to-morrow ;
But not a mortal love can know,
   But he must taste of sorrow.

For love comes here, and love goes there,
   For love is coy and fickle.
How often will he shun the fair,
   And yet the ugly tickle.

XLIX.

LOVE SONG.

OH love ! who can thy sway deny ?
    Who can withstand thy dart ?
Who feels no thrill, who heaves no sigh
    With thy shaft in his heart ?
More strong than chains is woman's smile,
    For chains will break apart,
While love that's pure, and free from guile.
    Will never more depart.

Who hath a heart as hard as stone ?
    Who hath a breast like ice ?
Let woman's charms to him be known
    How soon these shall suffice.
That heart and breast shall soften, melt,
    Nor ever freeze again,
And only while love's joys are felt
    Shall it be free from pain.

www.ingramcontent.com/pod-product-compliance
Lightning Source LLC
Chambersburg PA
CBHW020545270326
41927CB00006B/725